Flamingo Coloring Book

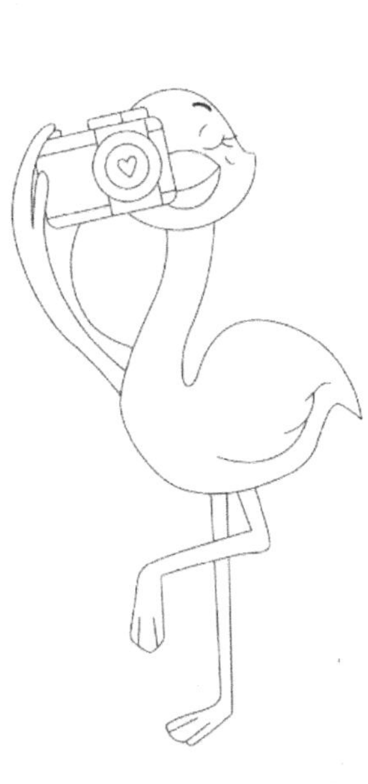

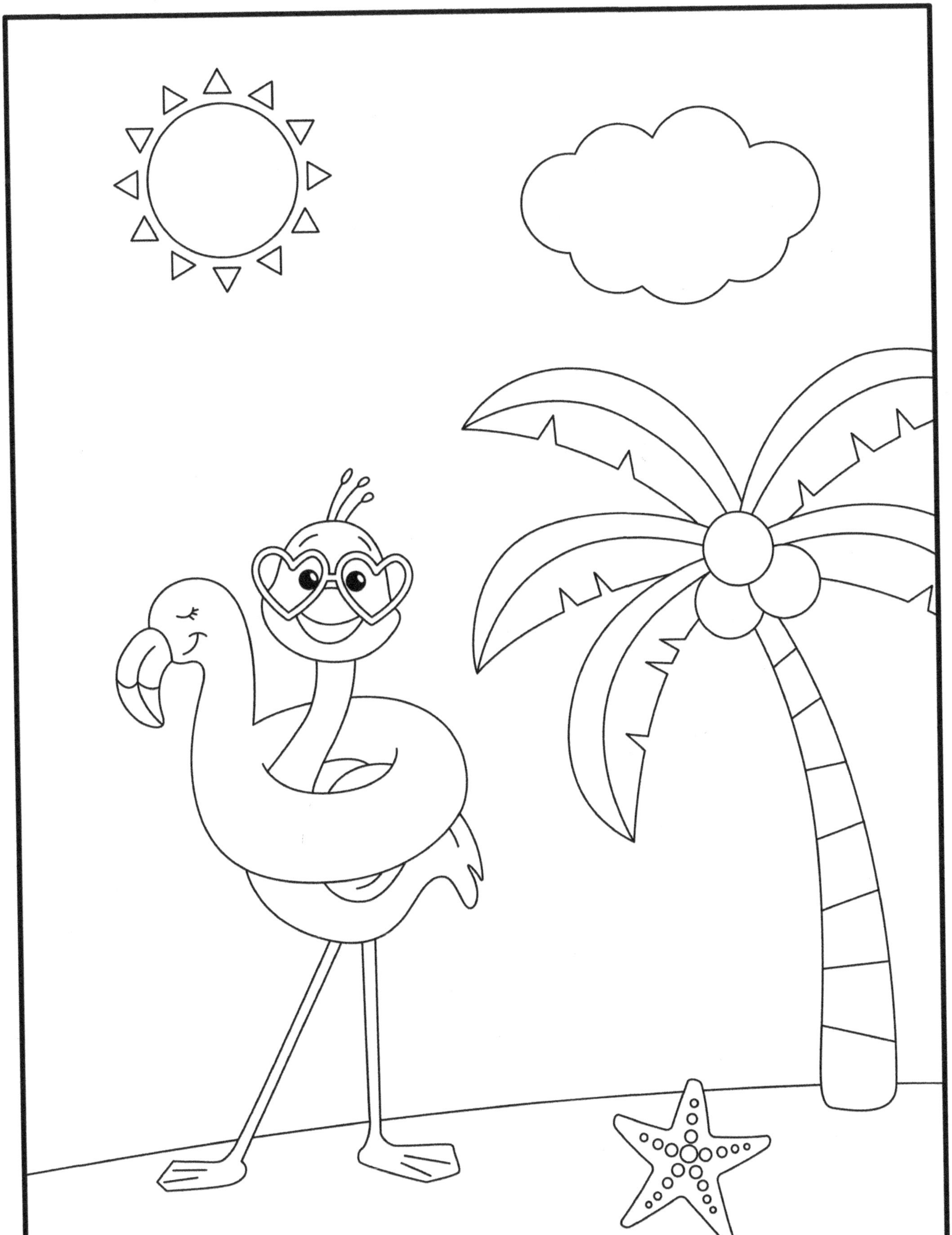

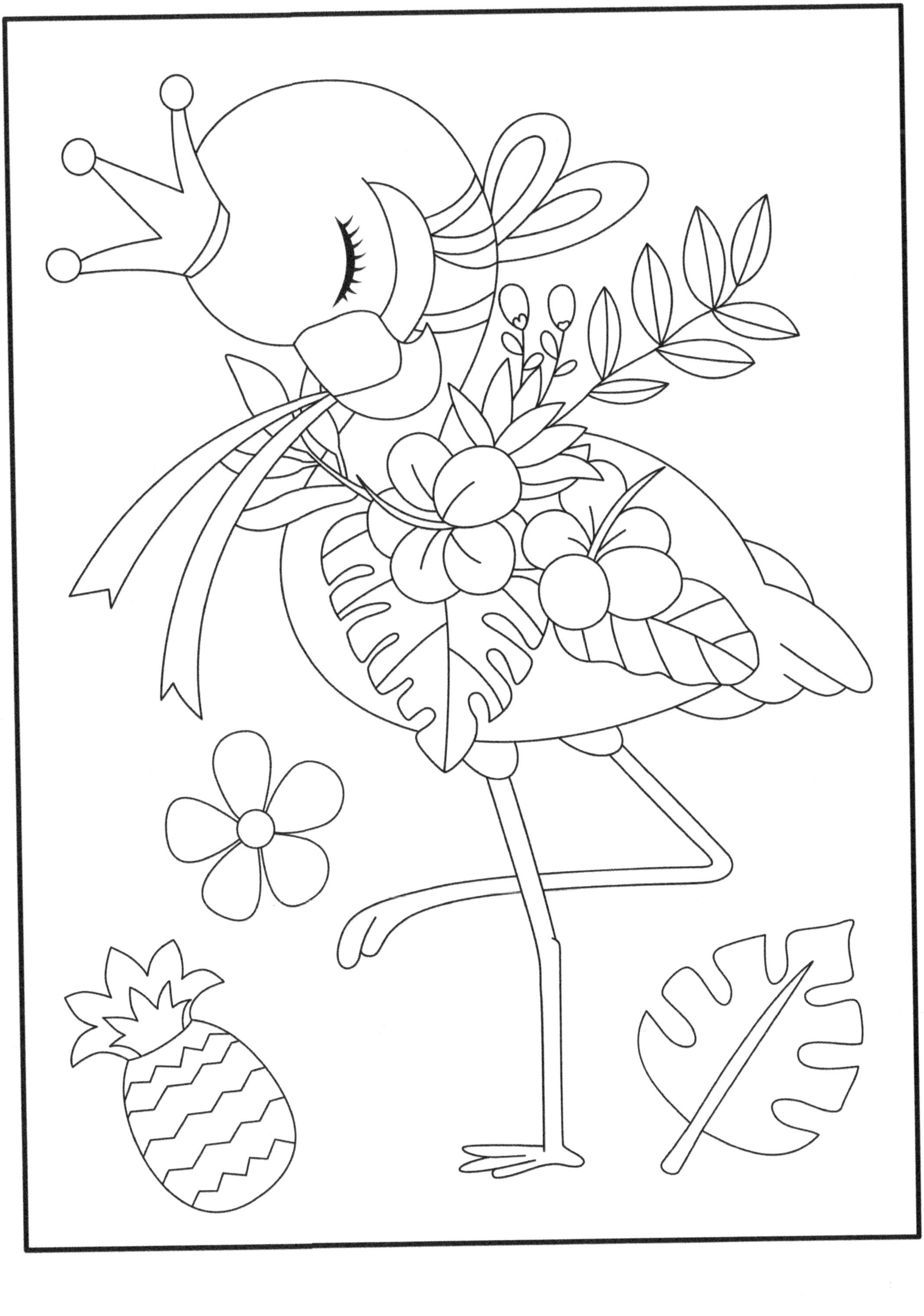

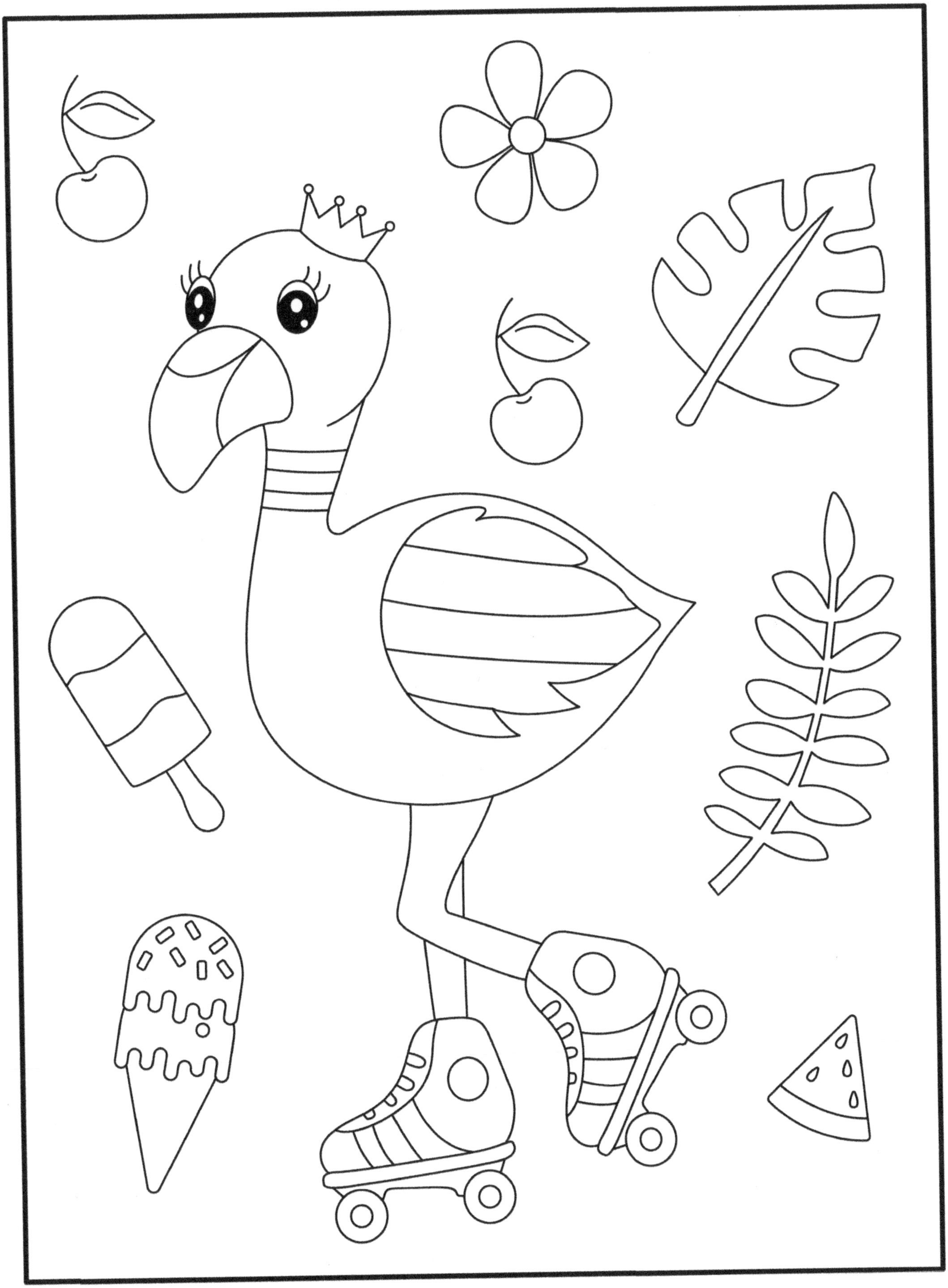

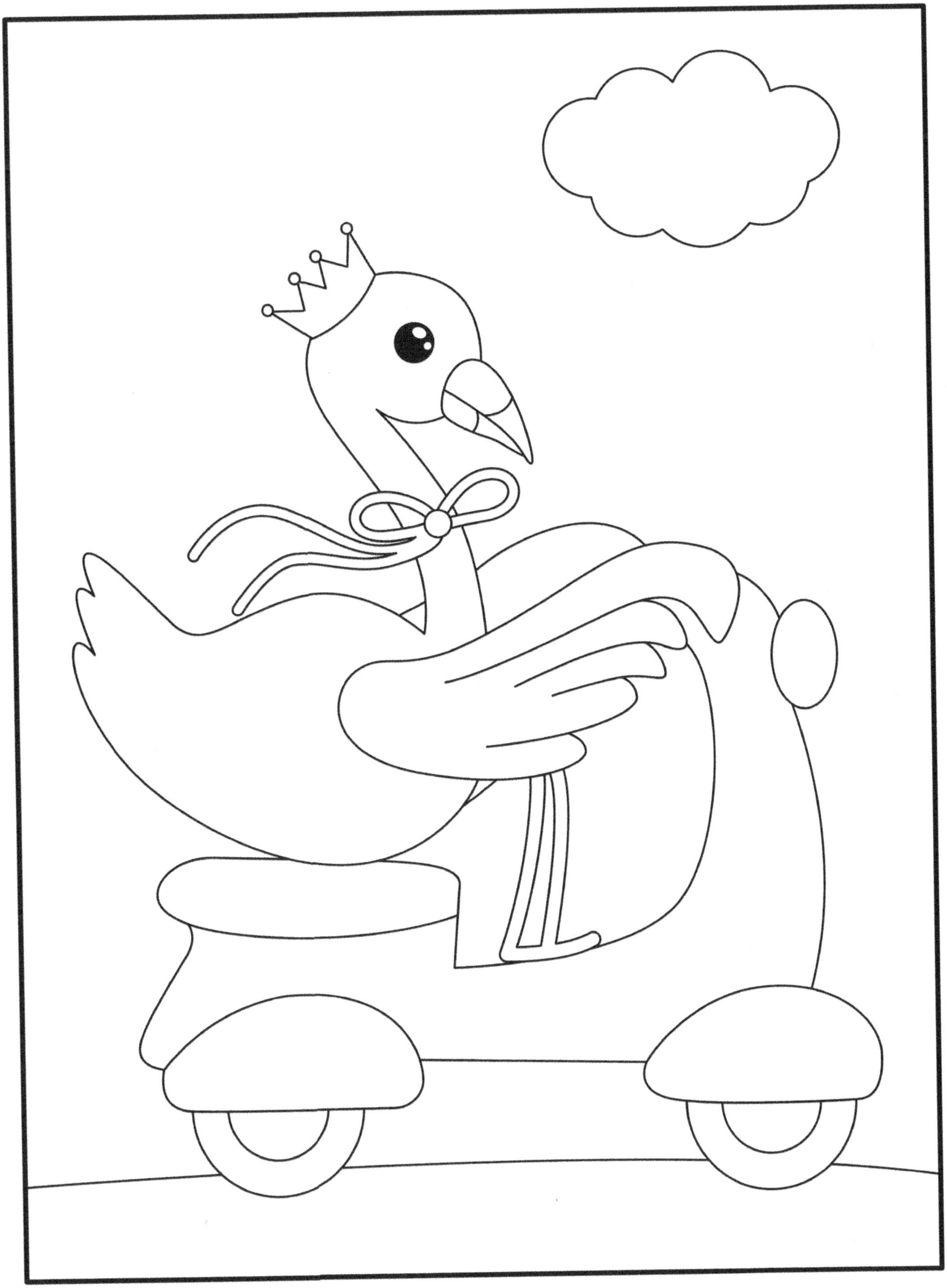

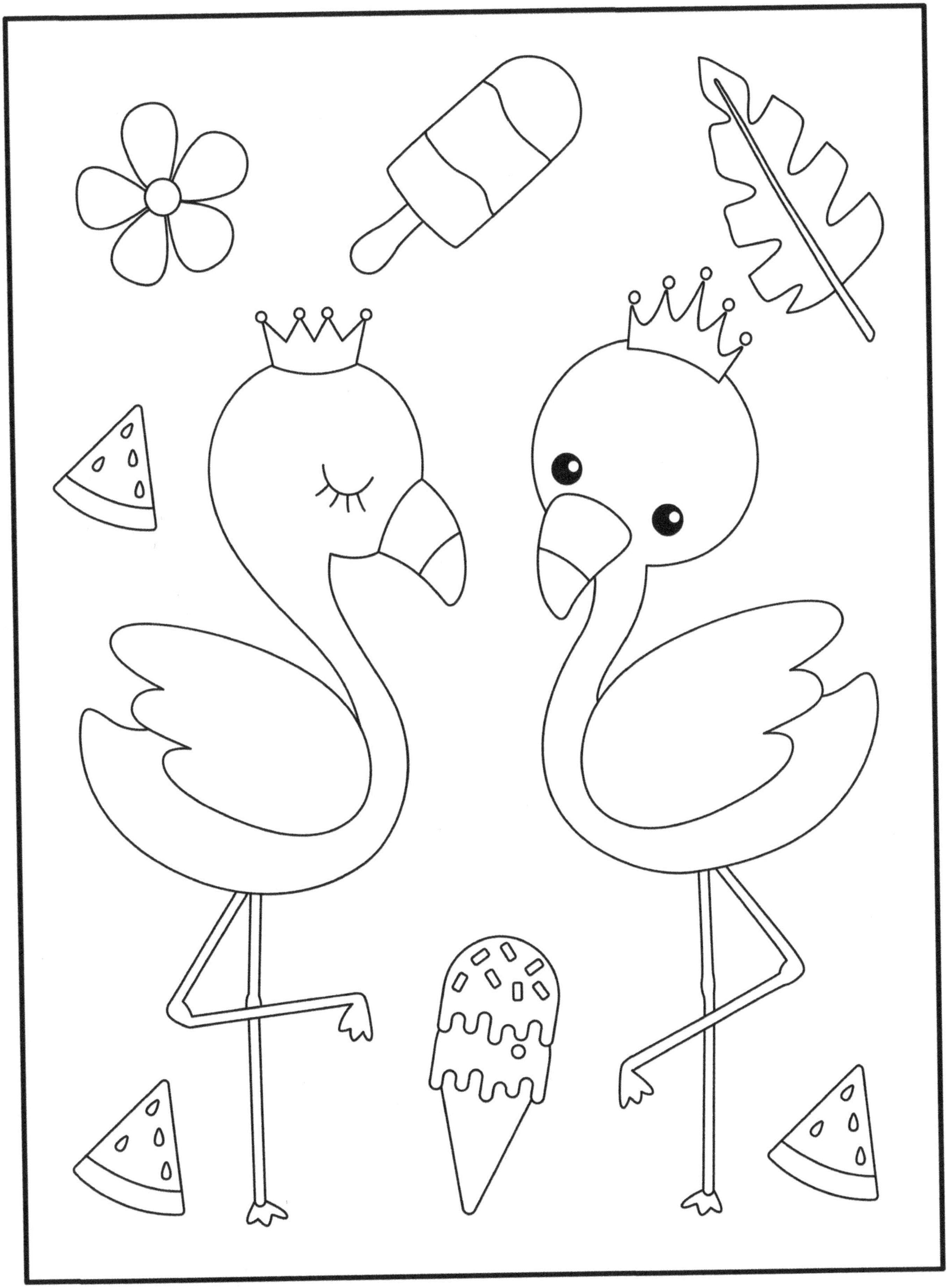

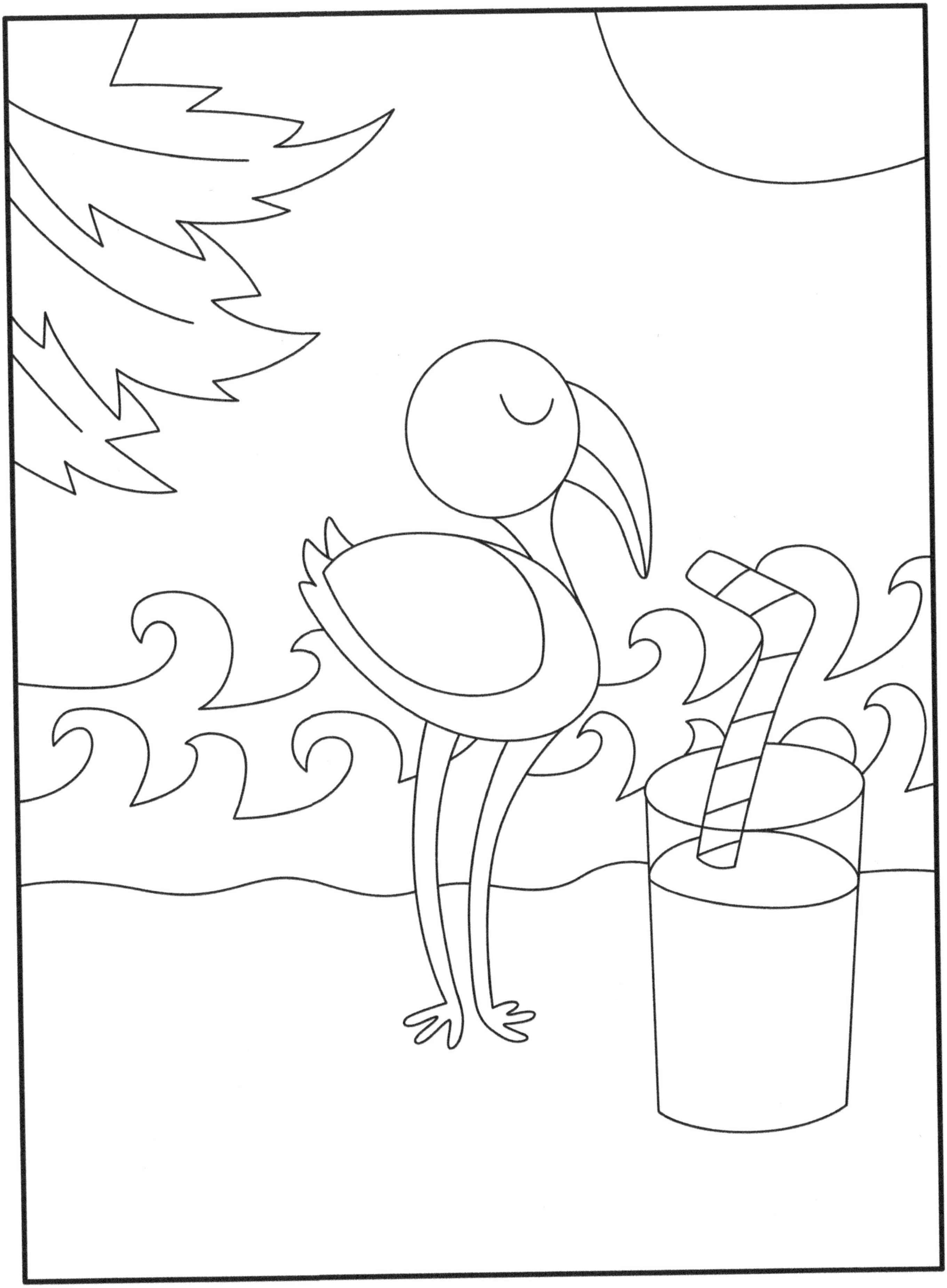

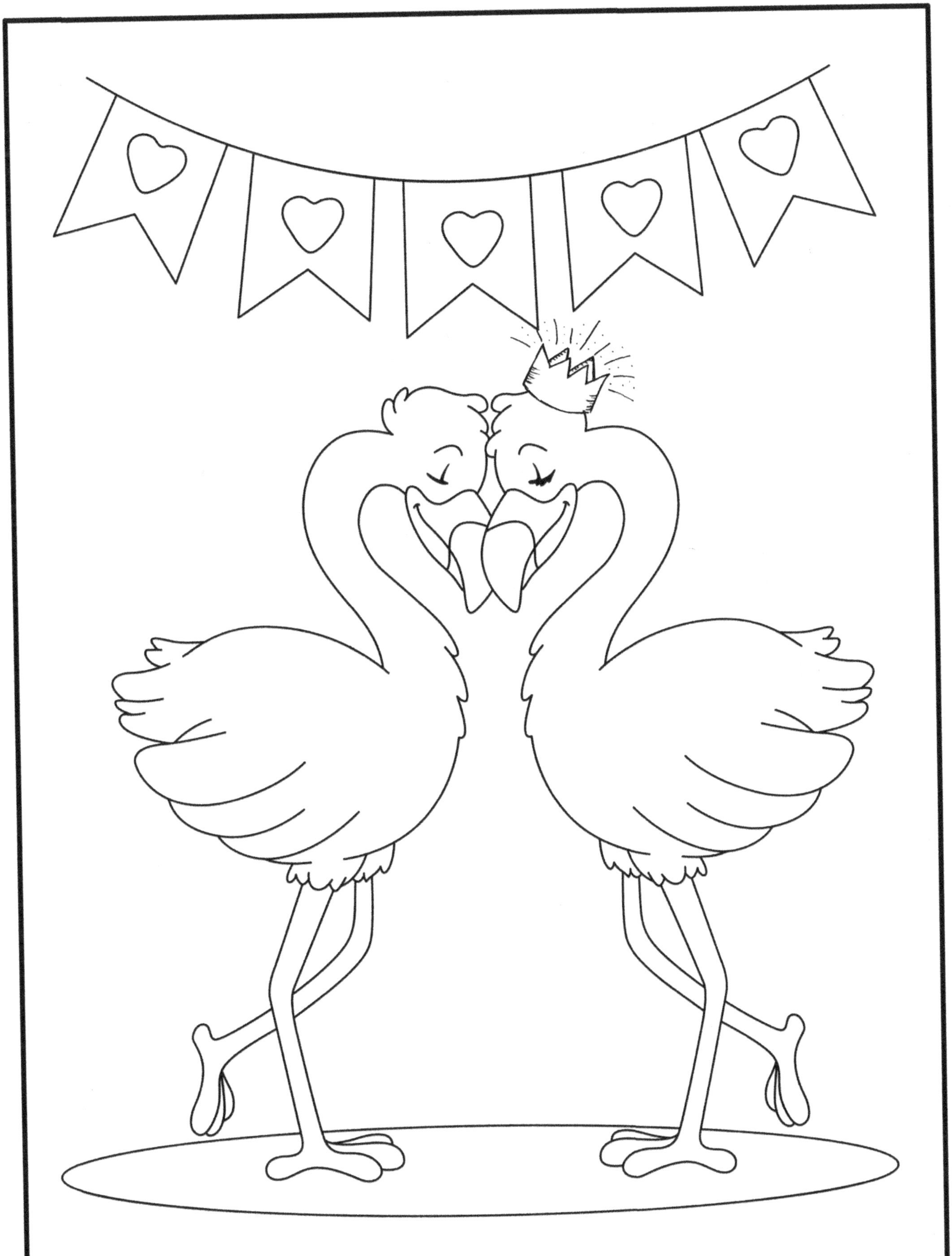

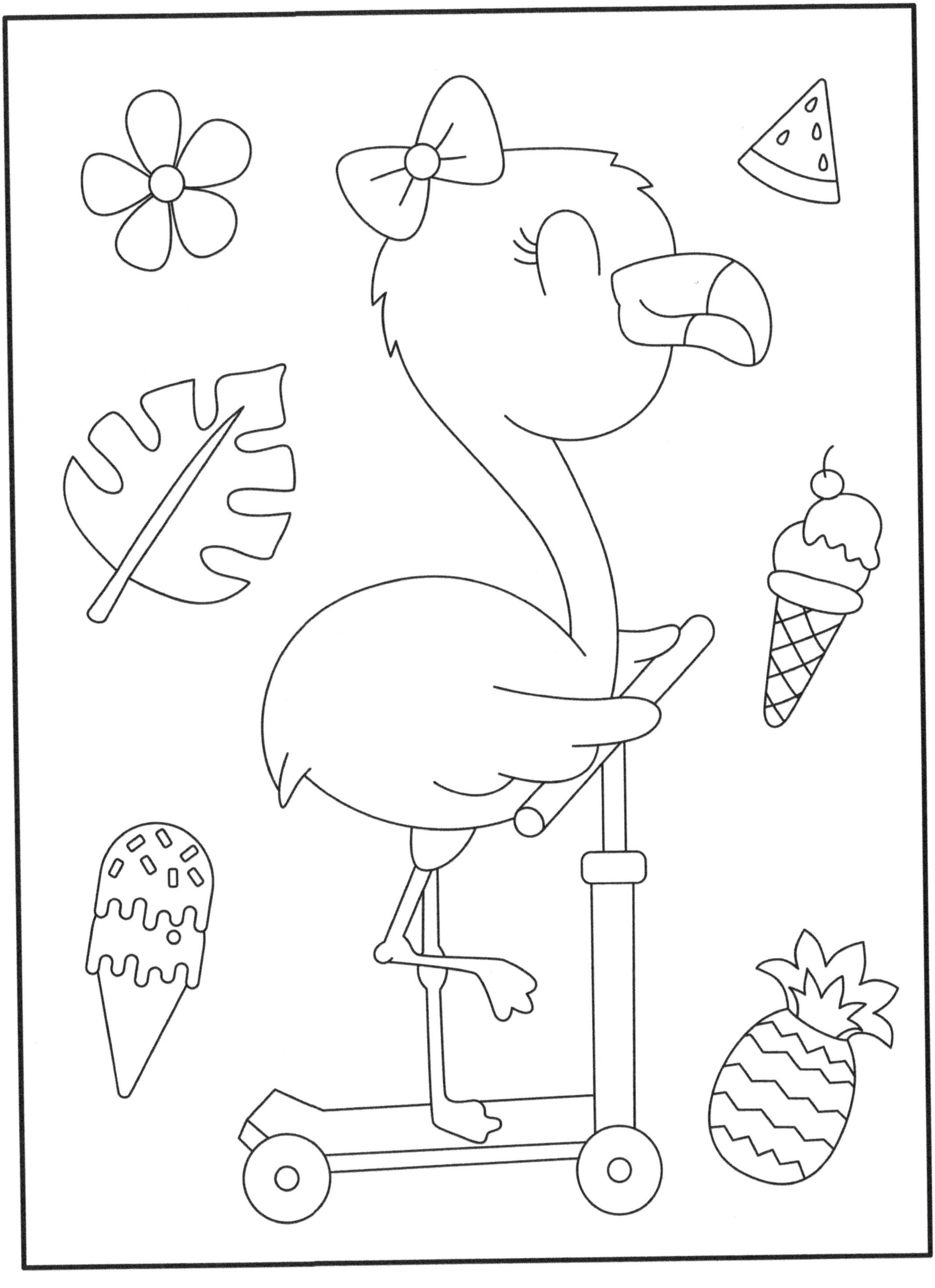

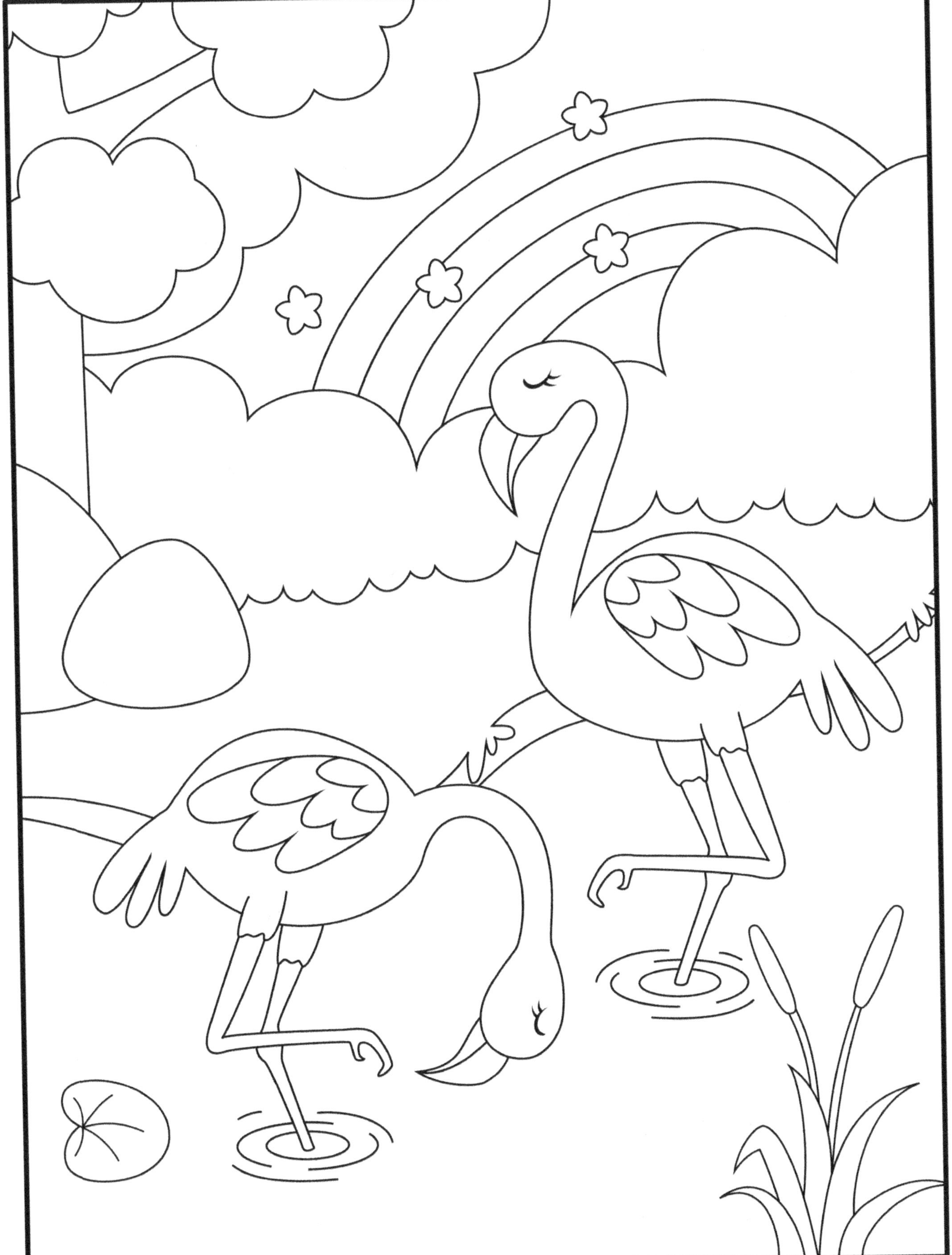

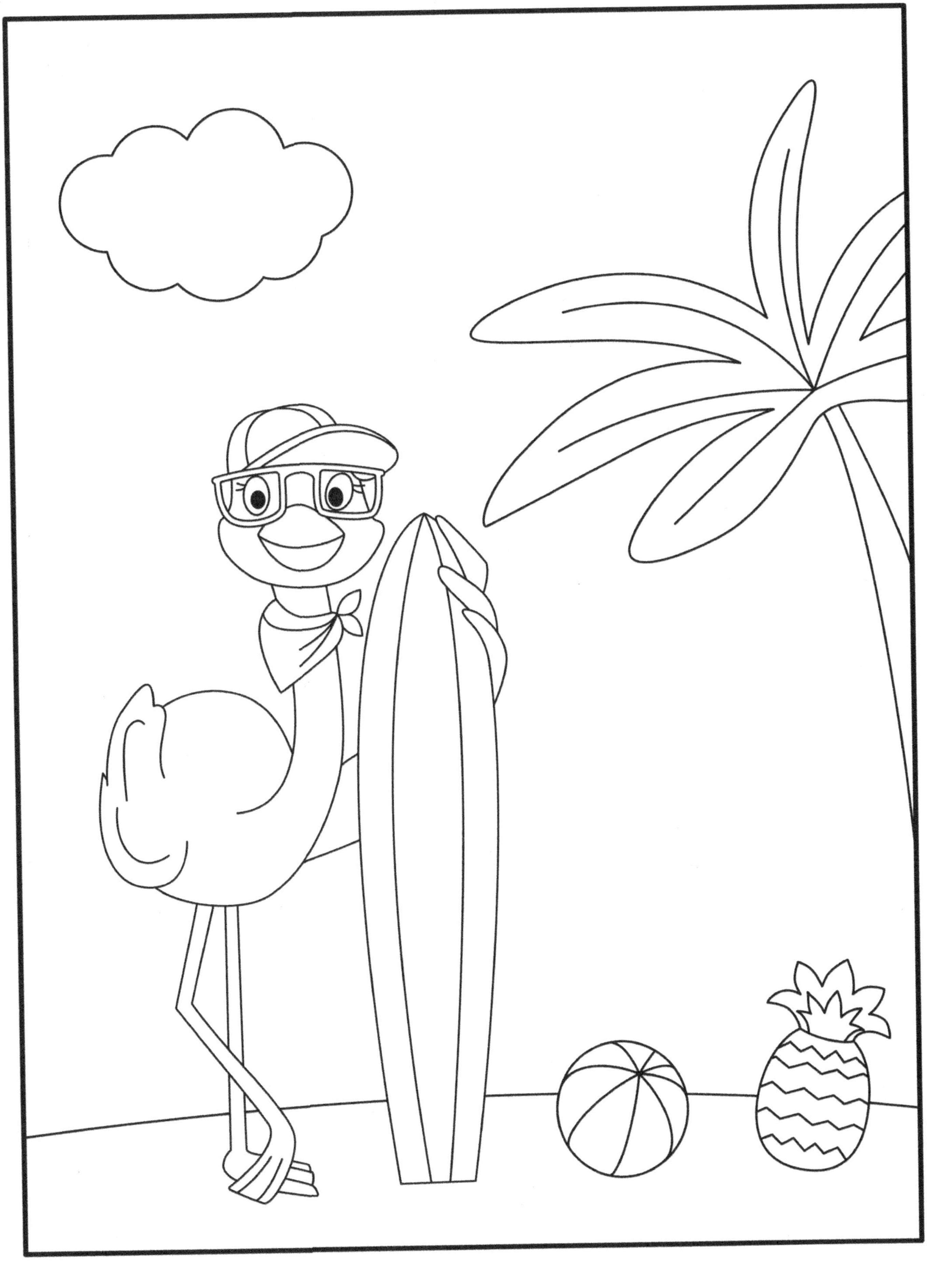

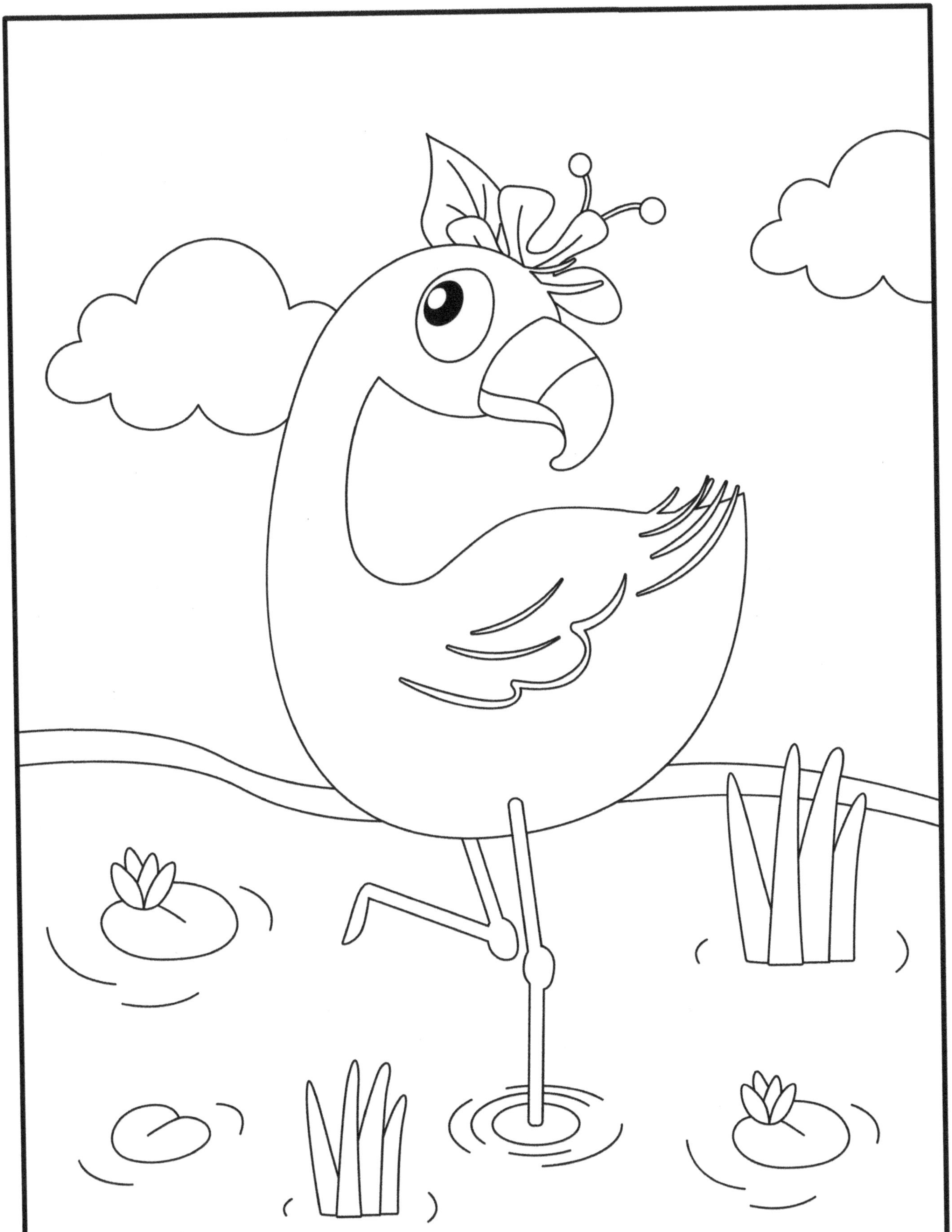

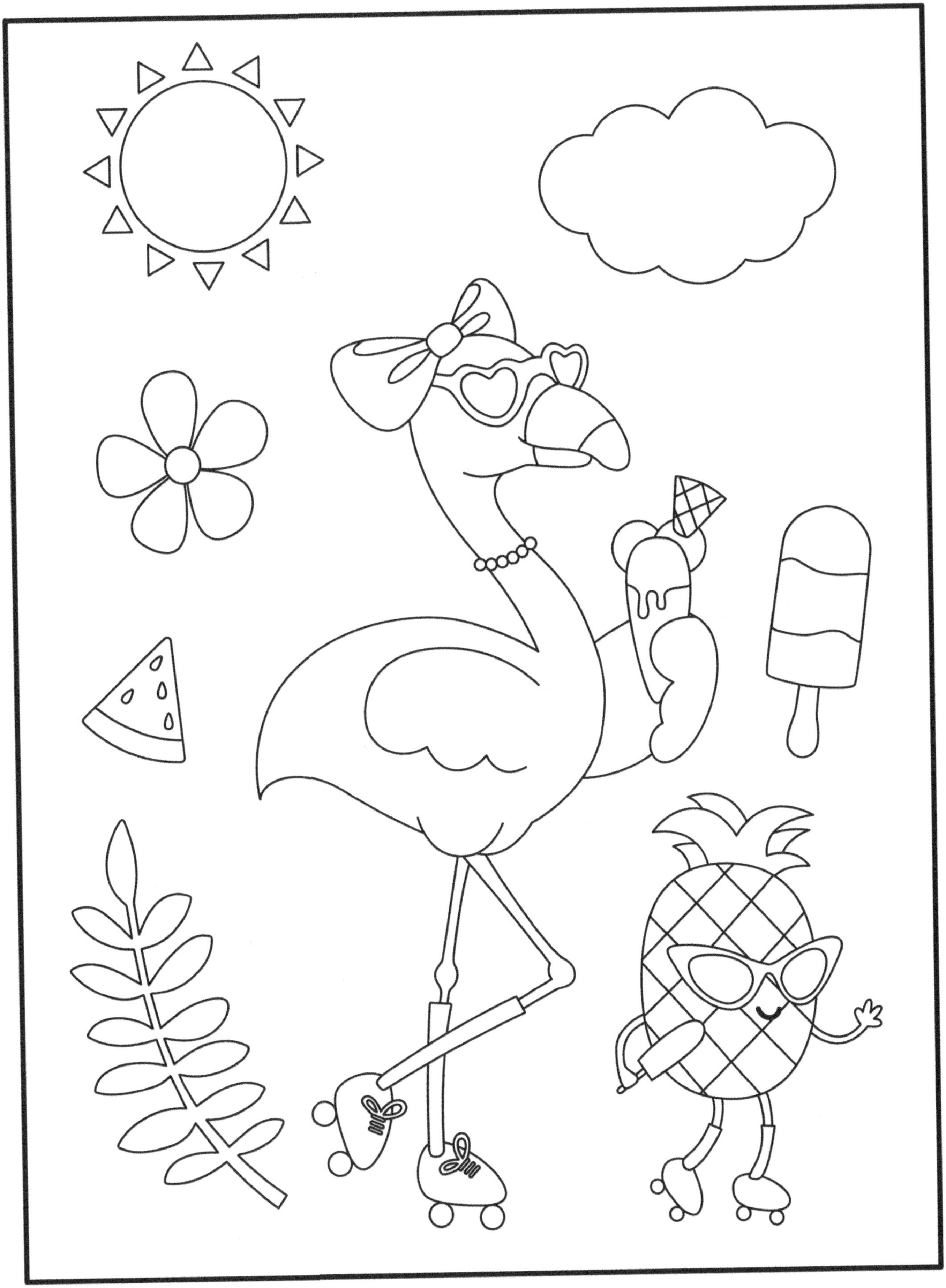

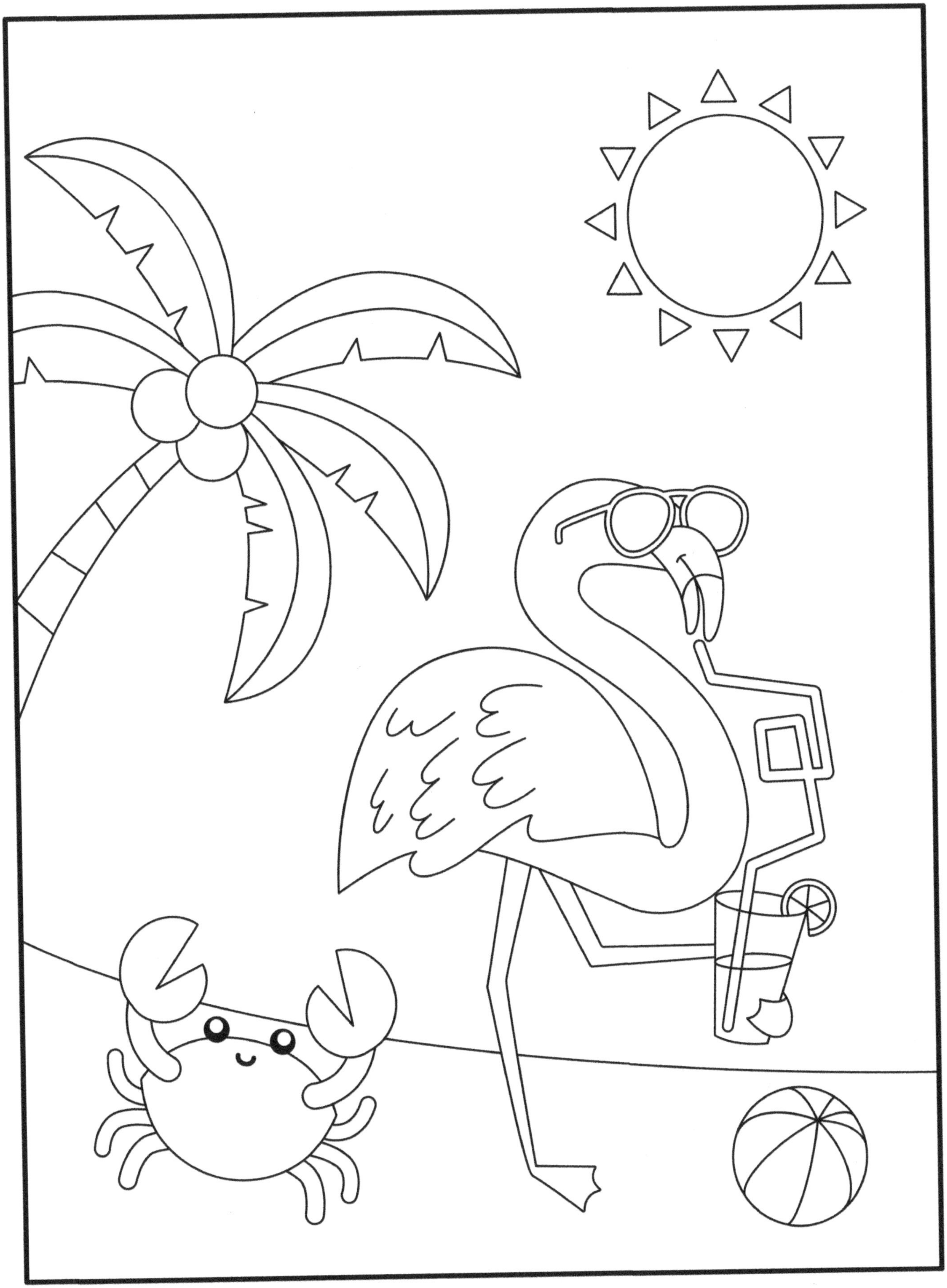

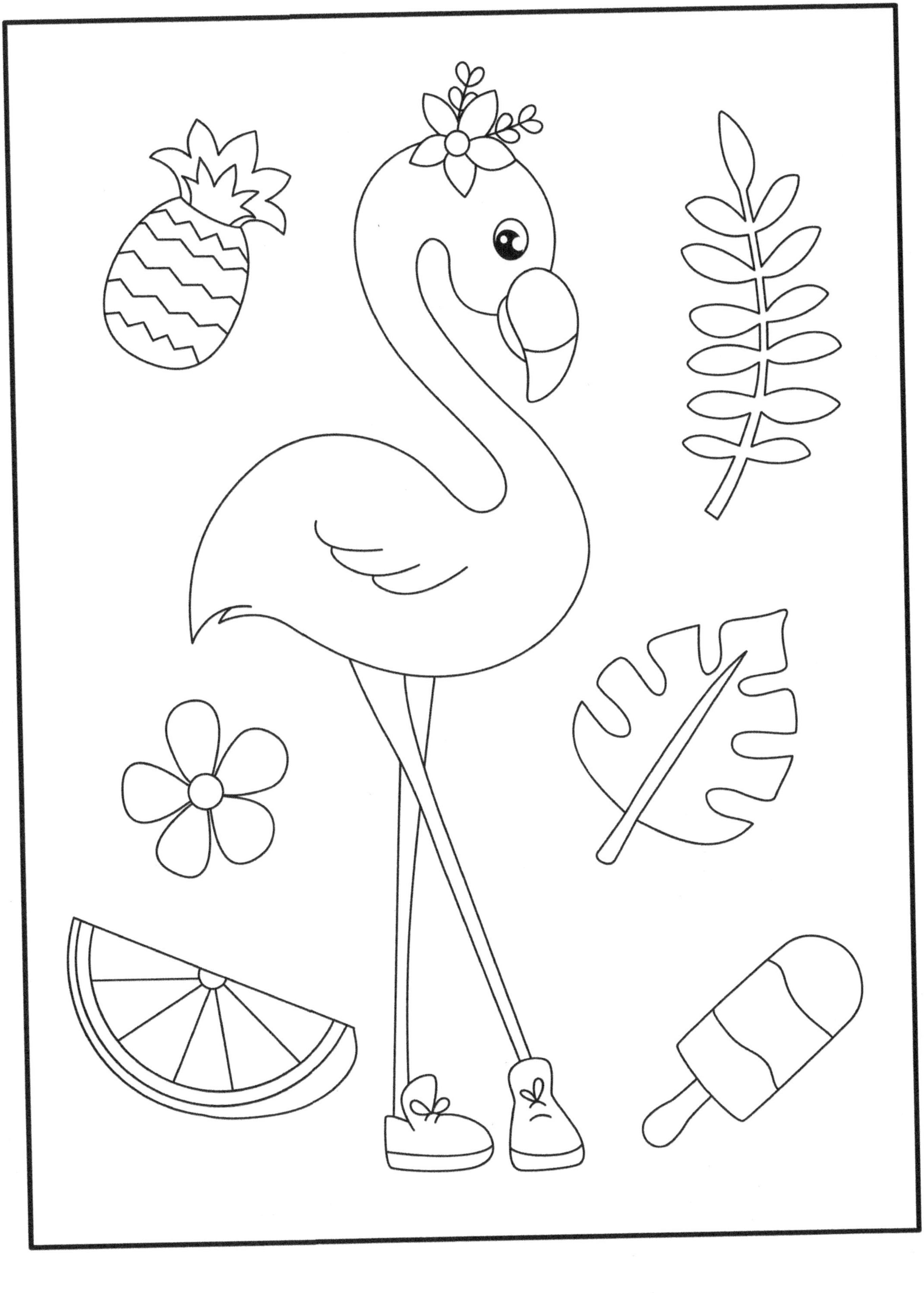

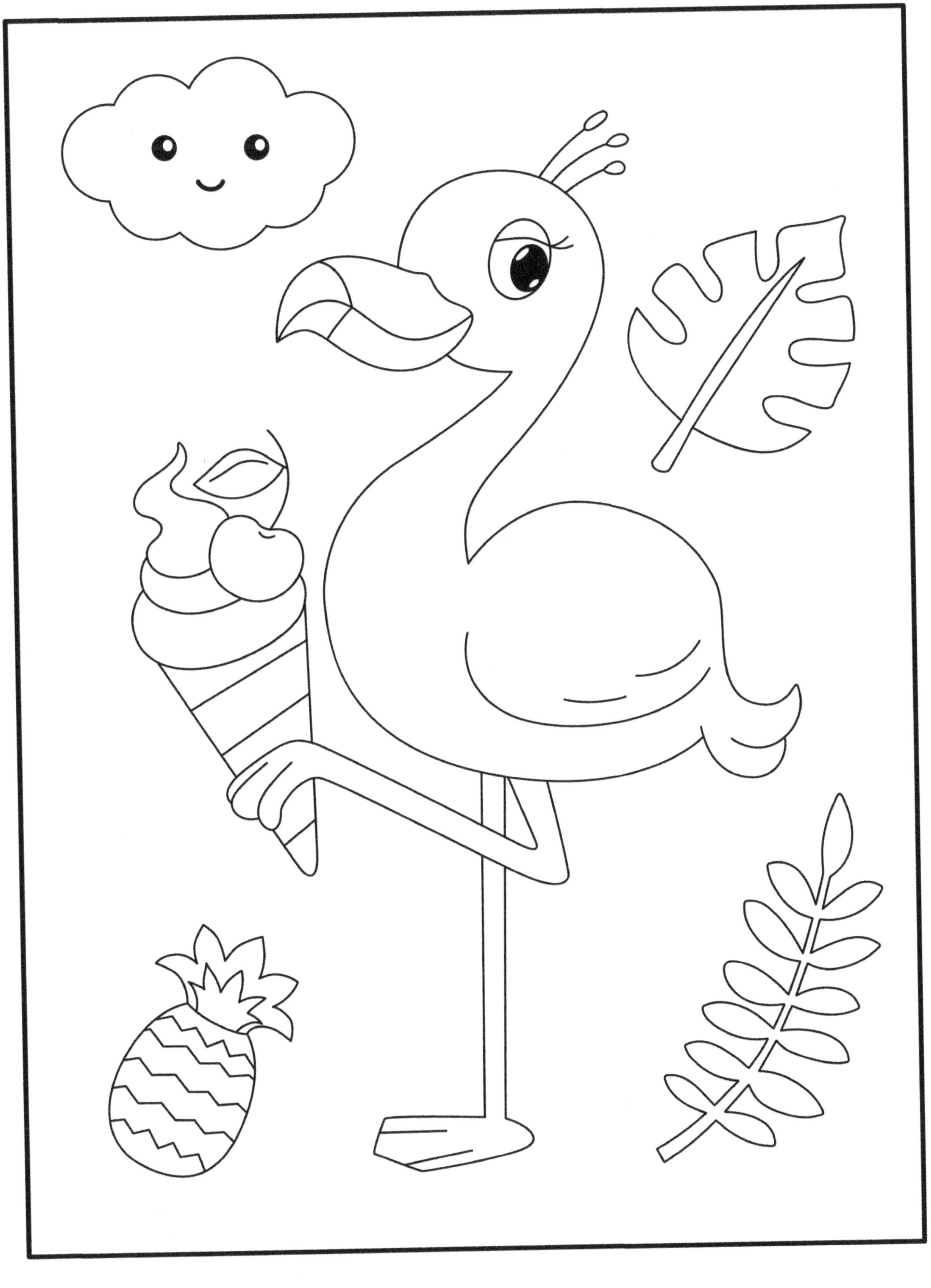

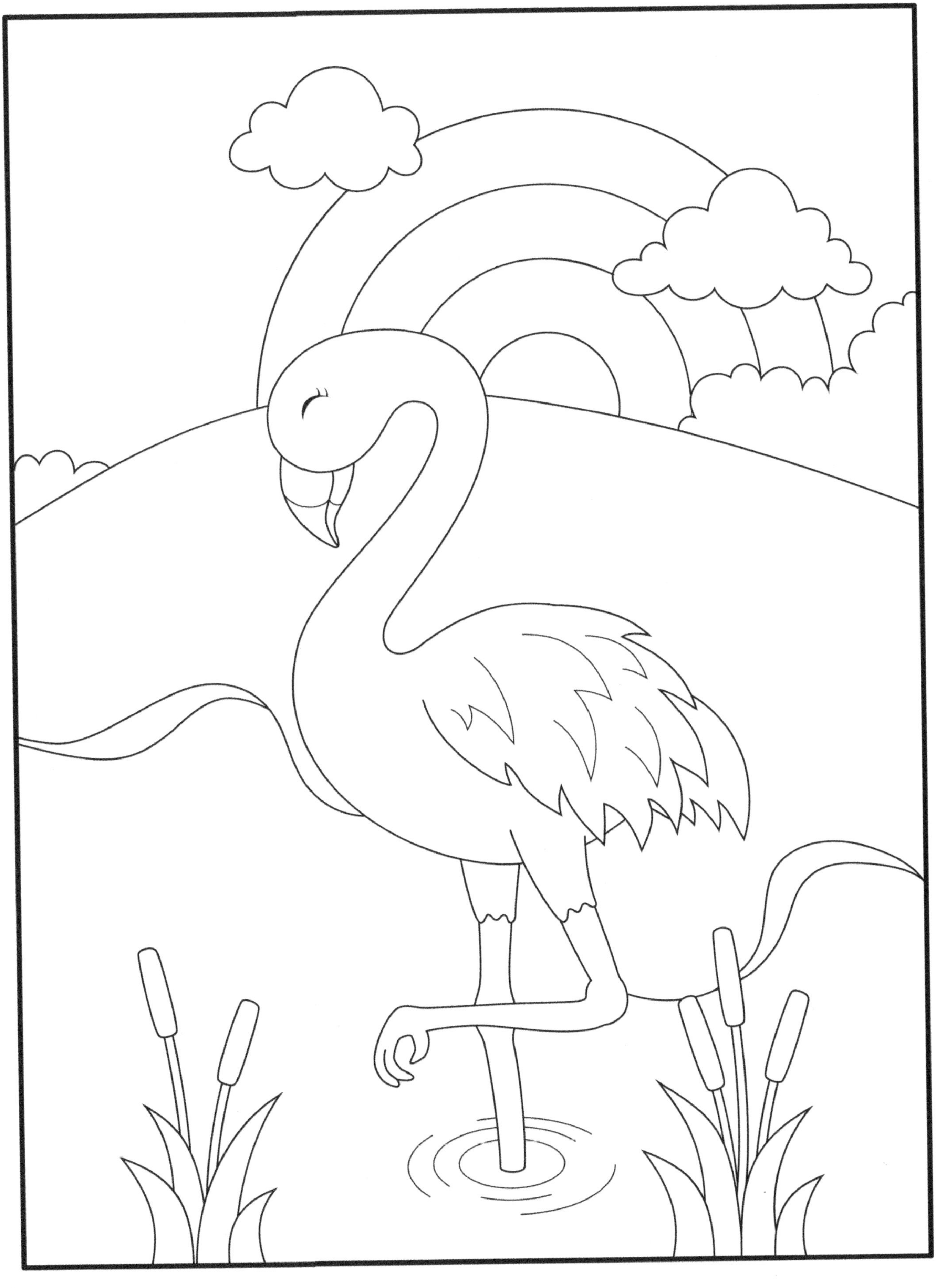

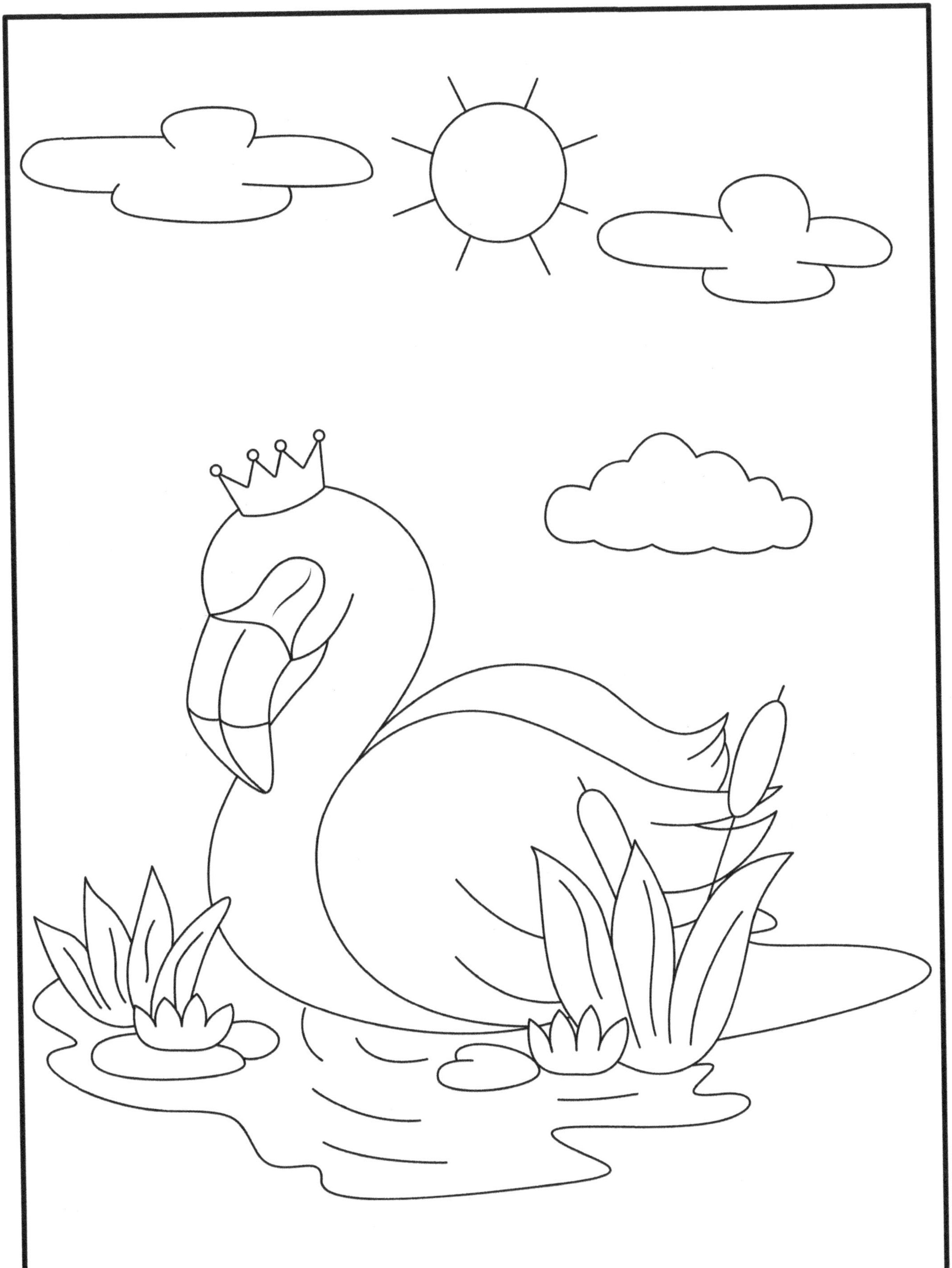

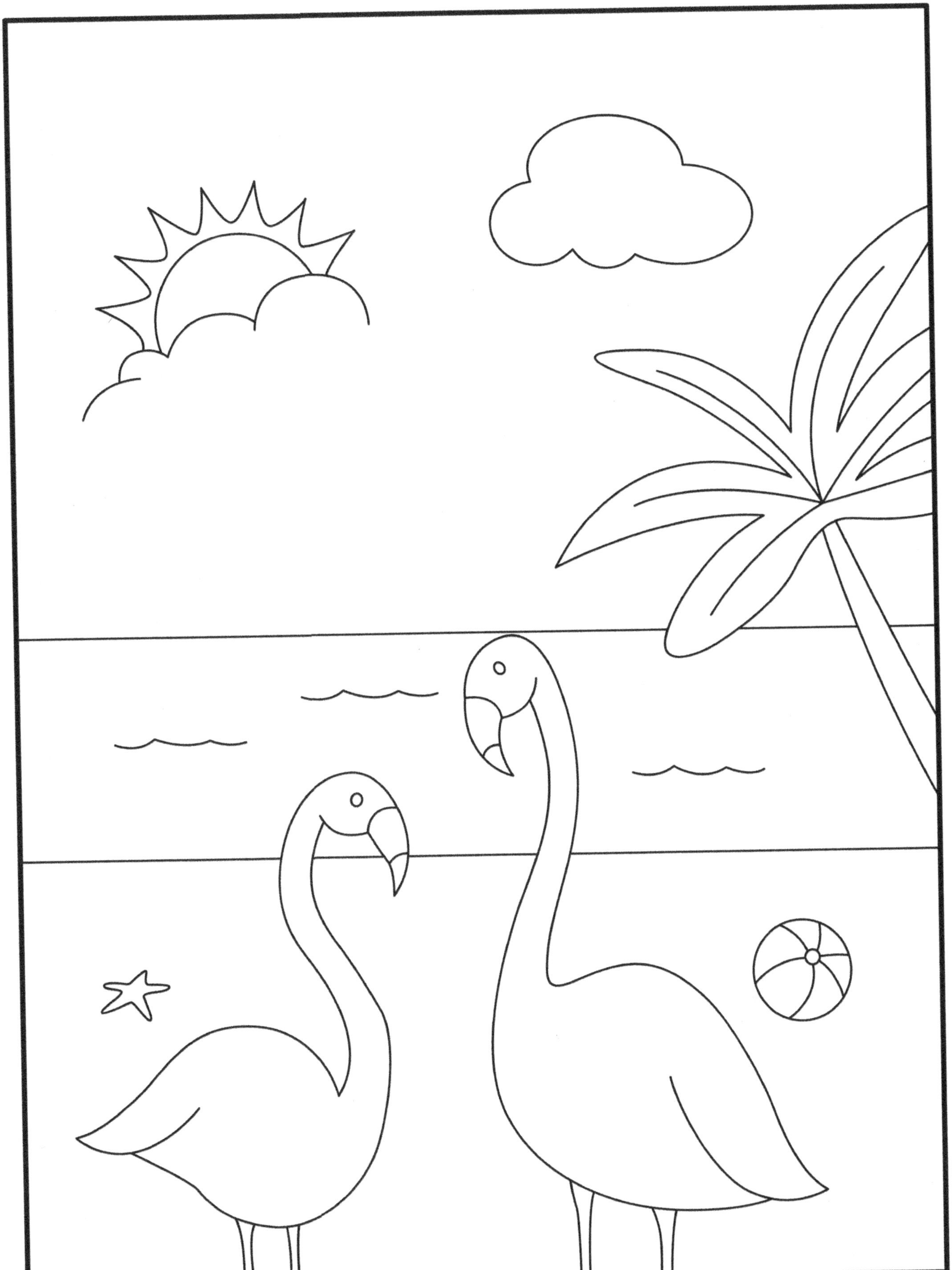

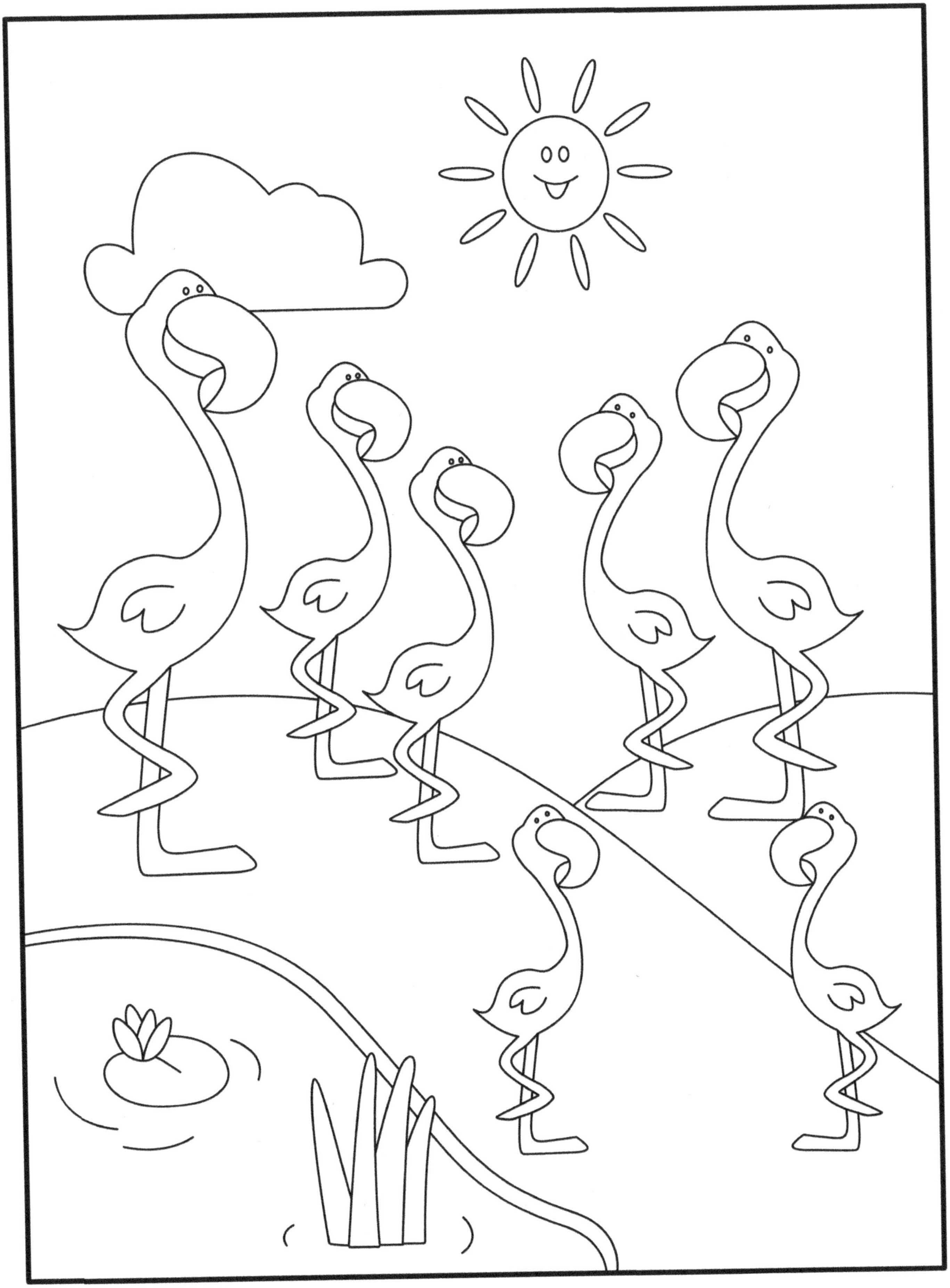

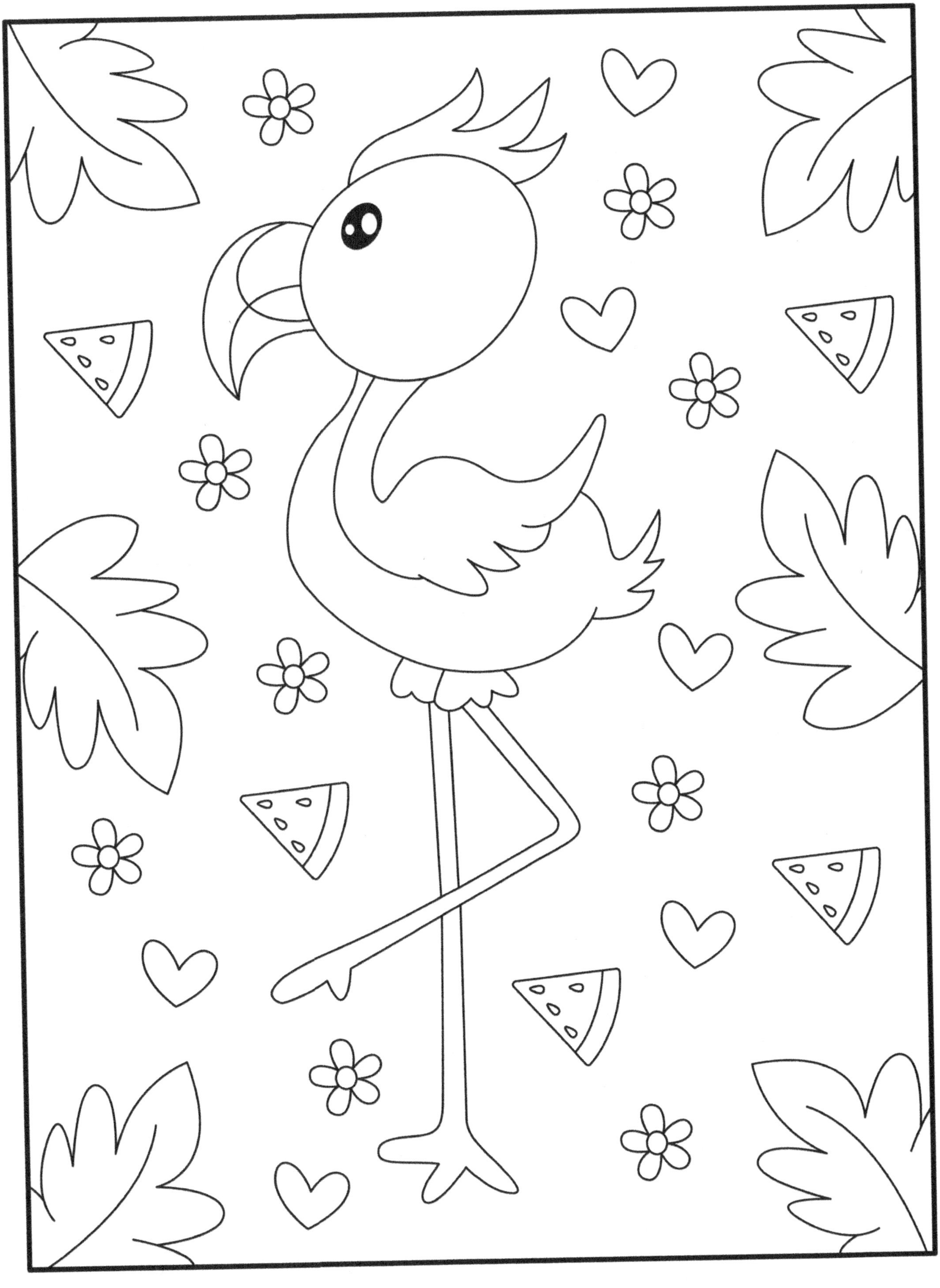

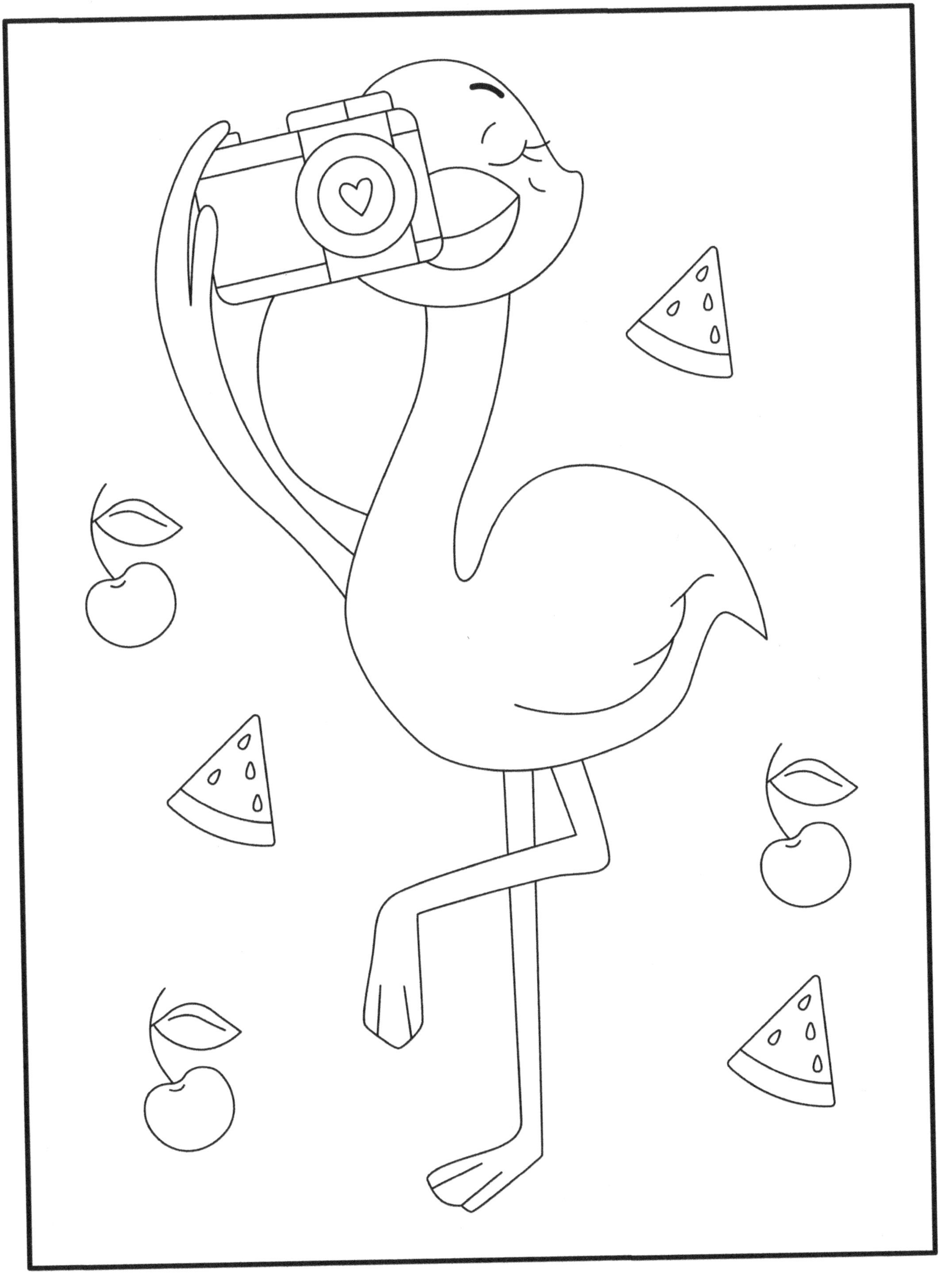

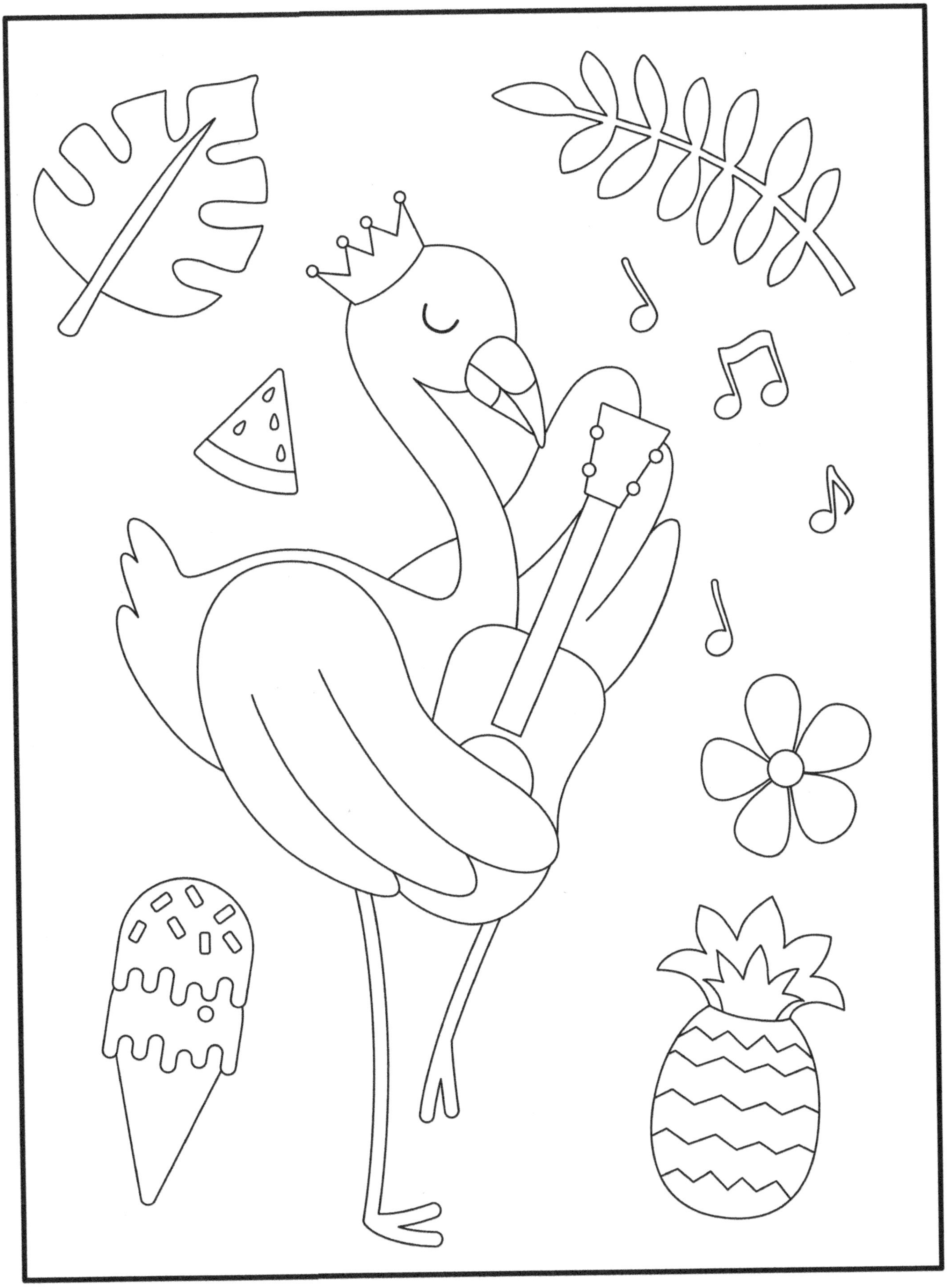

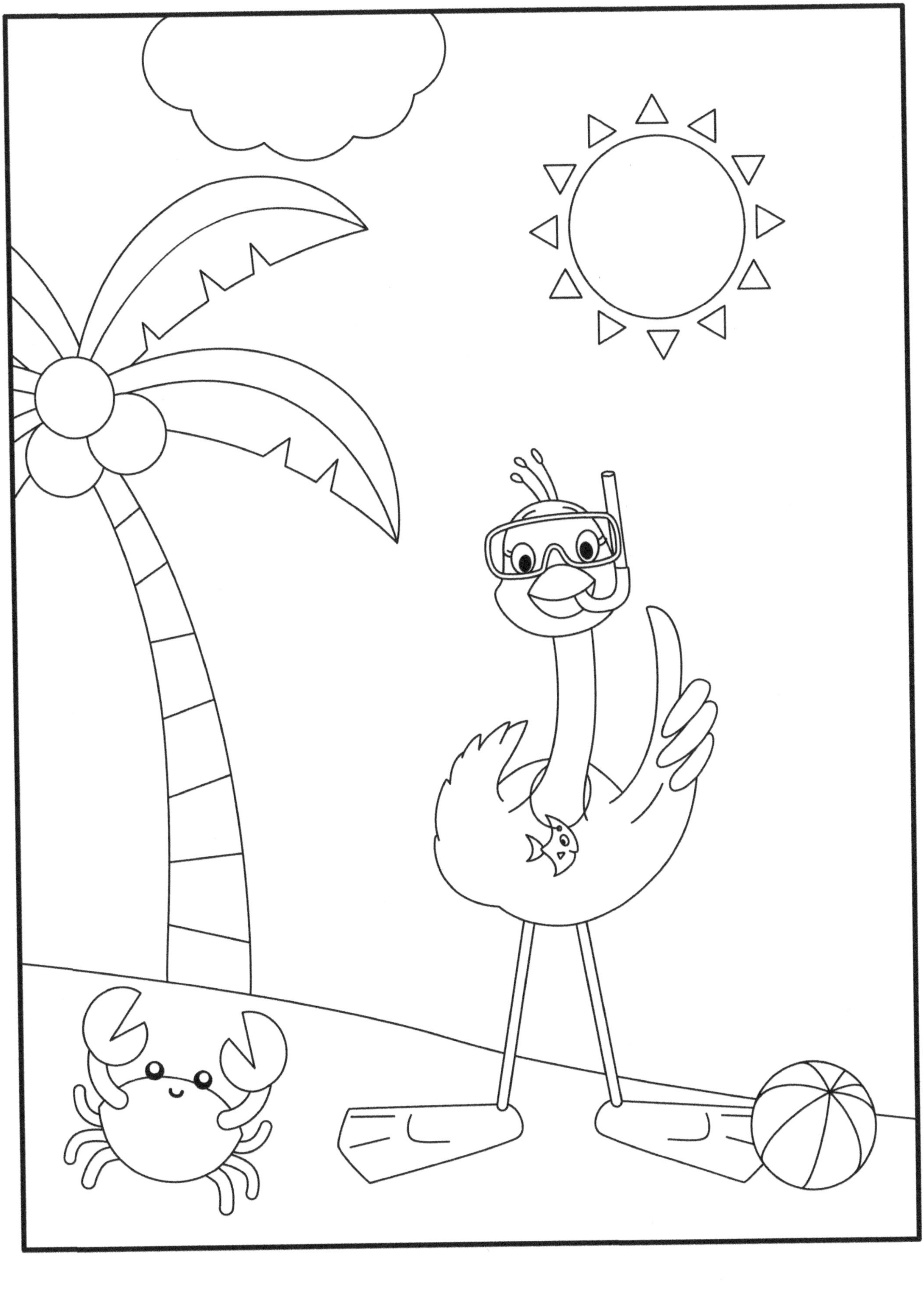

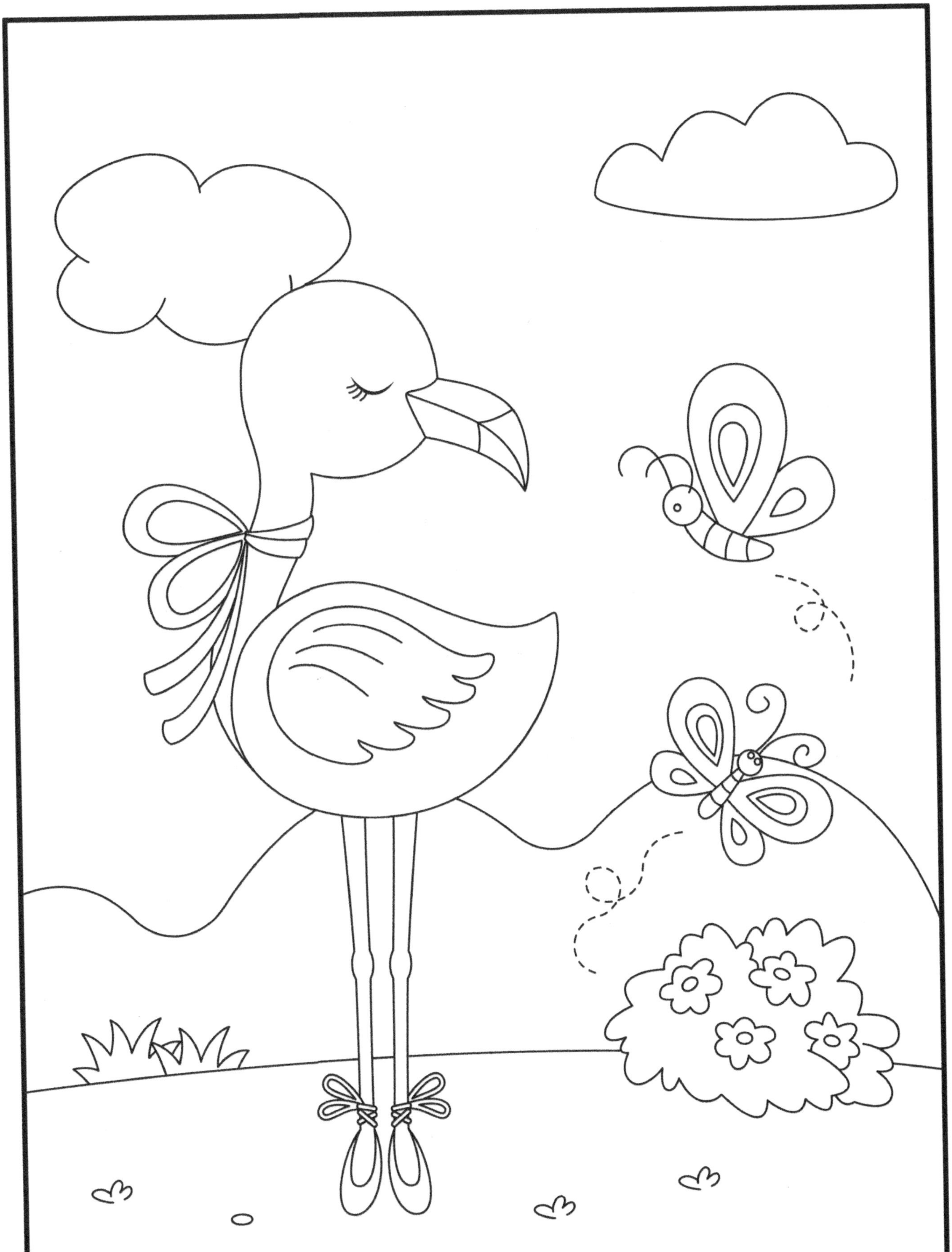

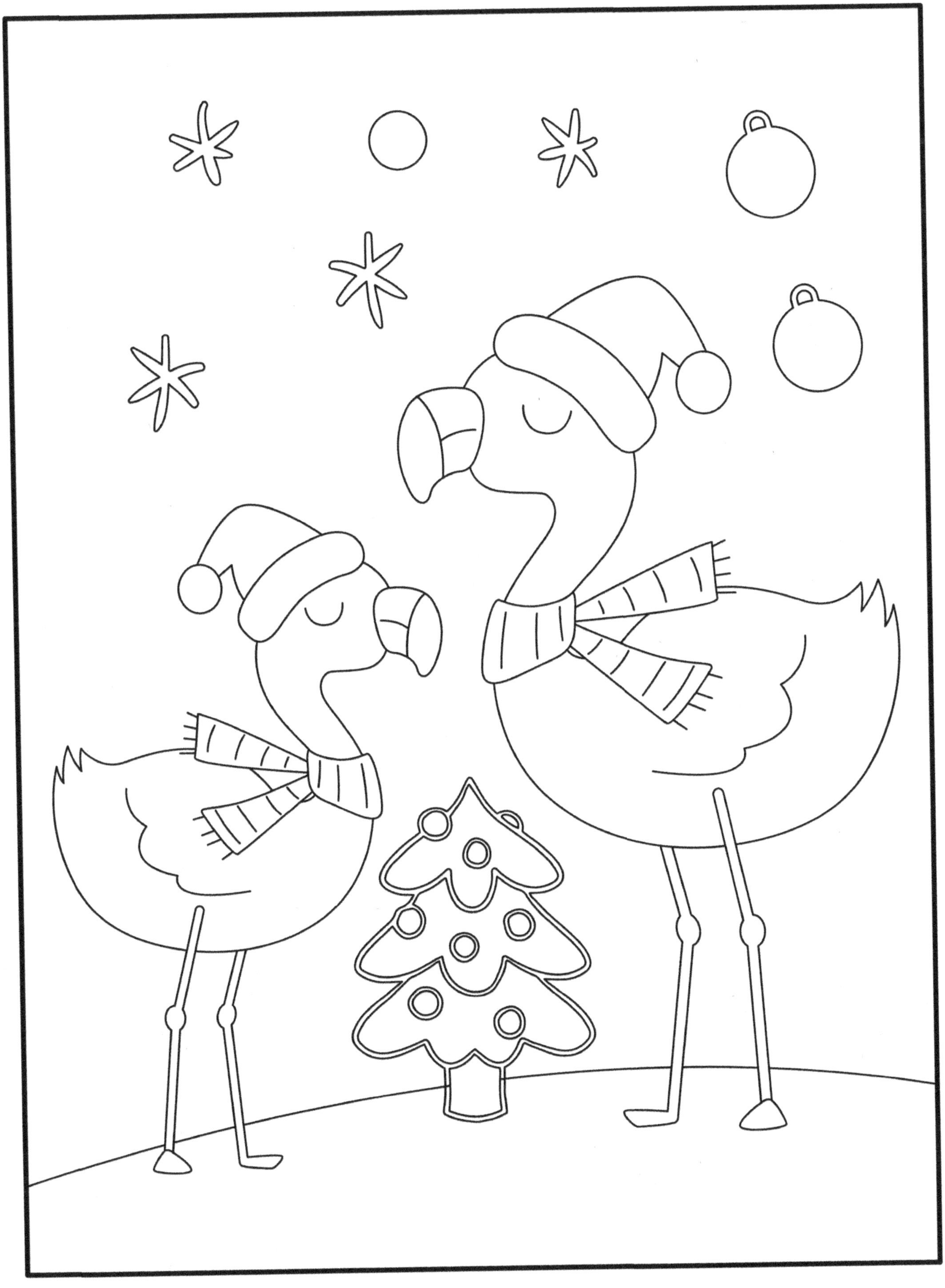

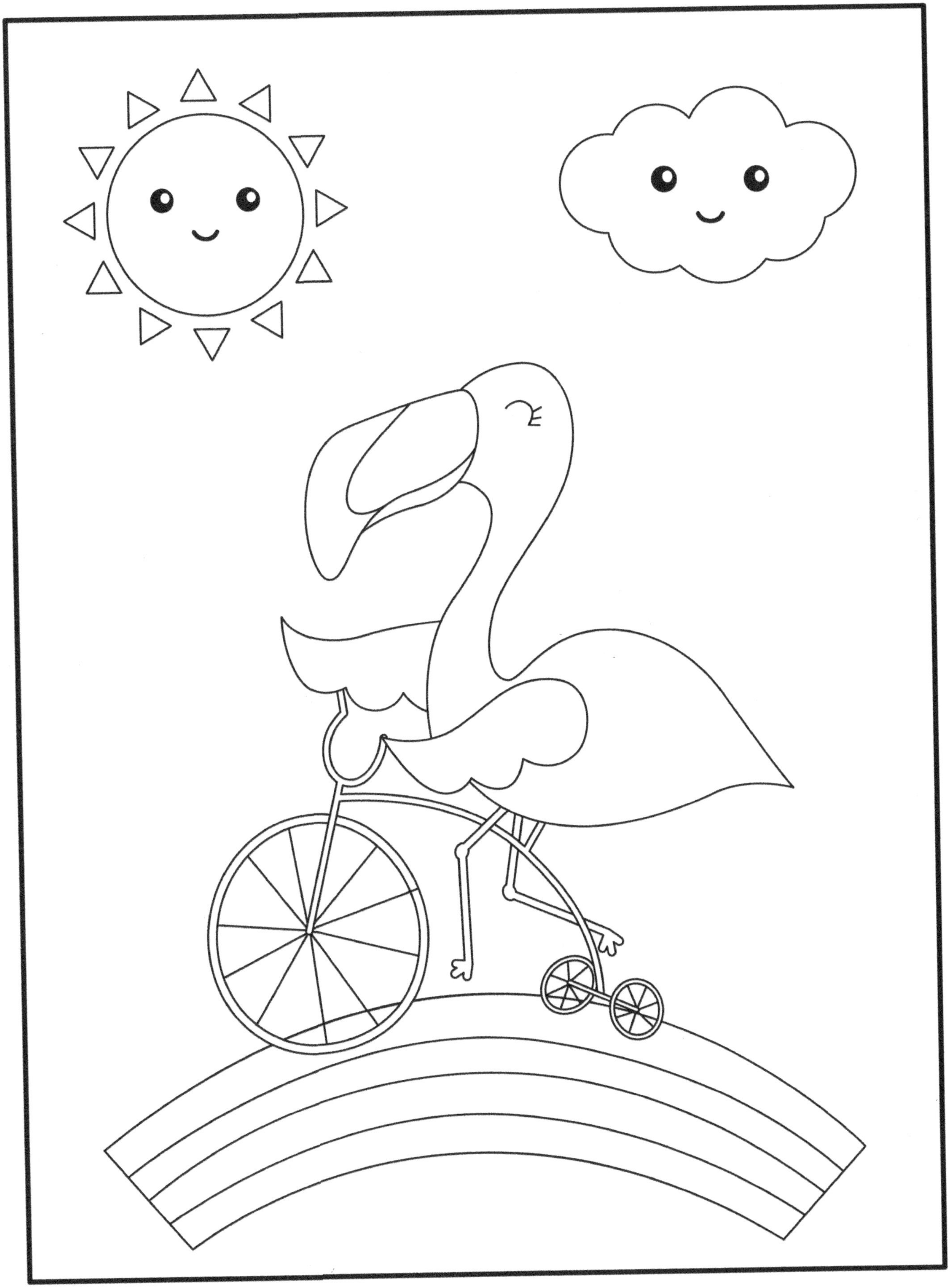

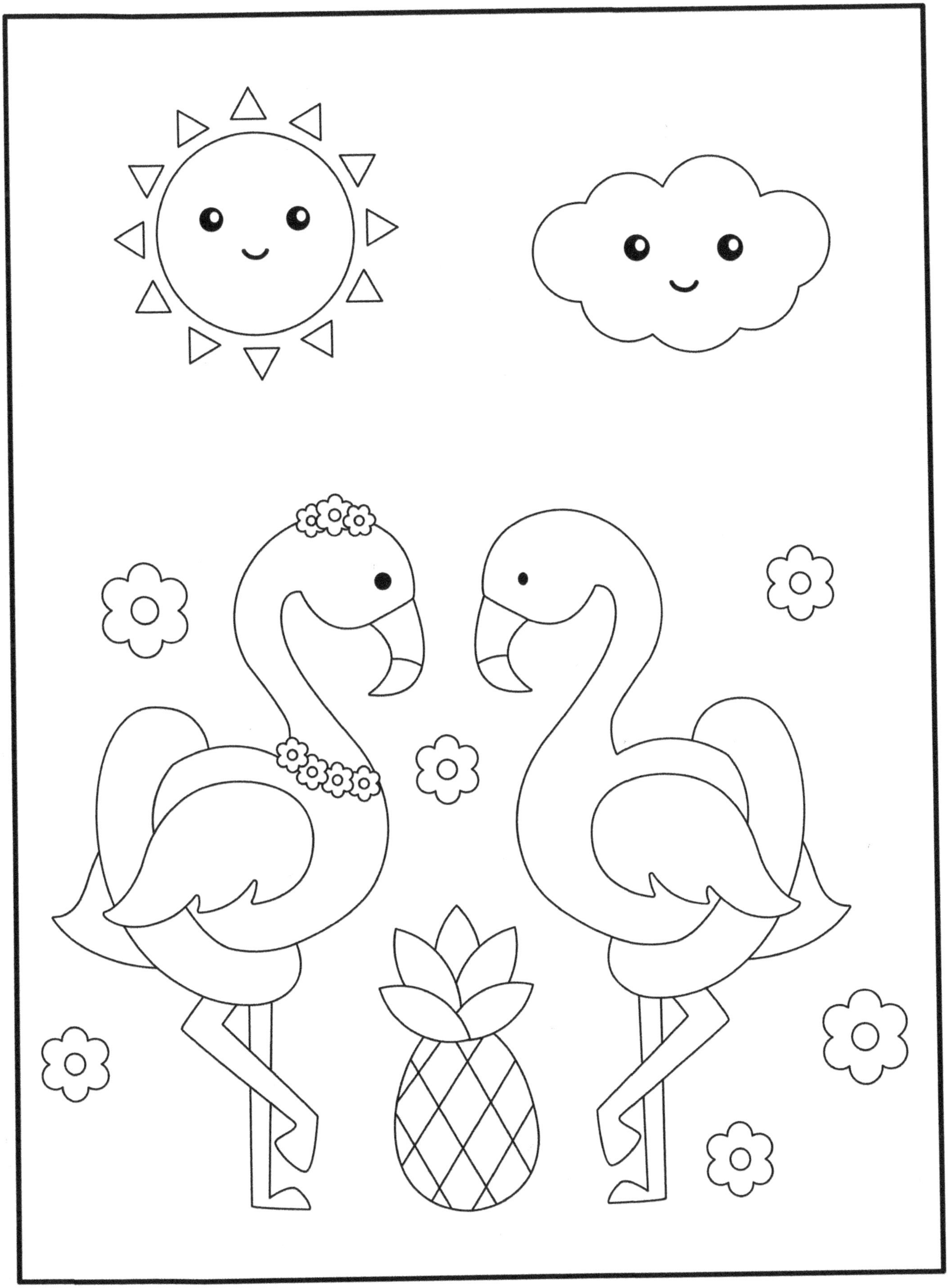

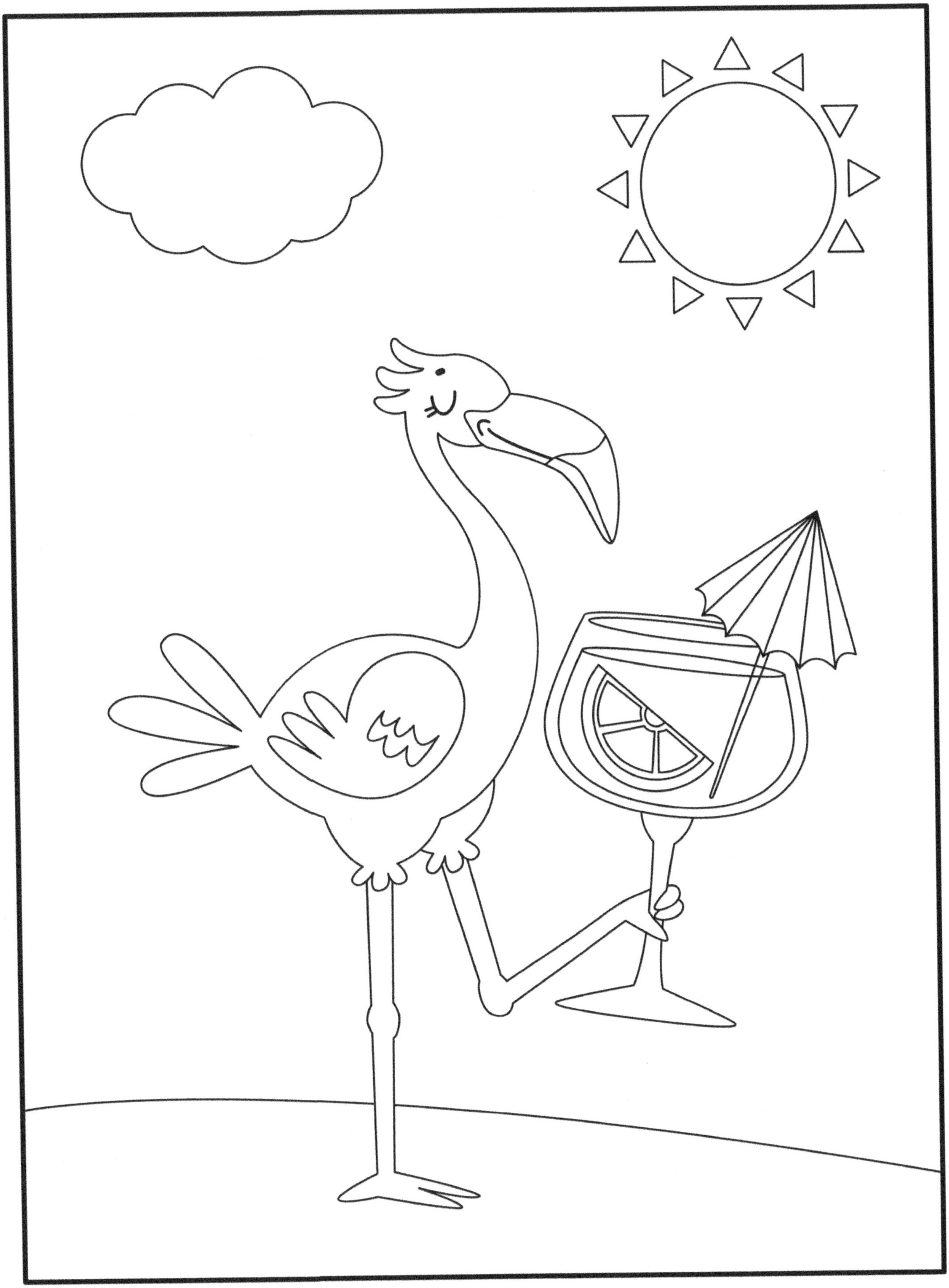

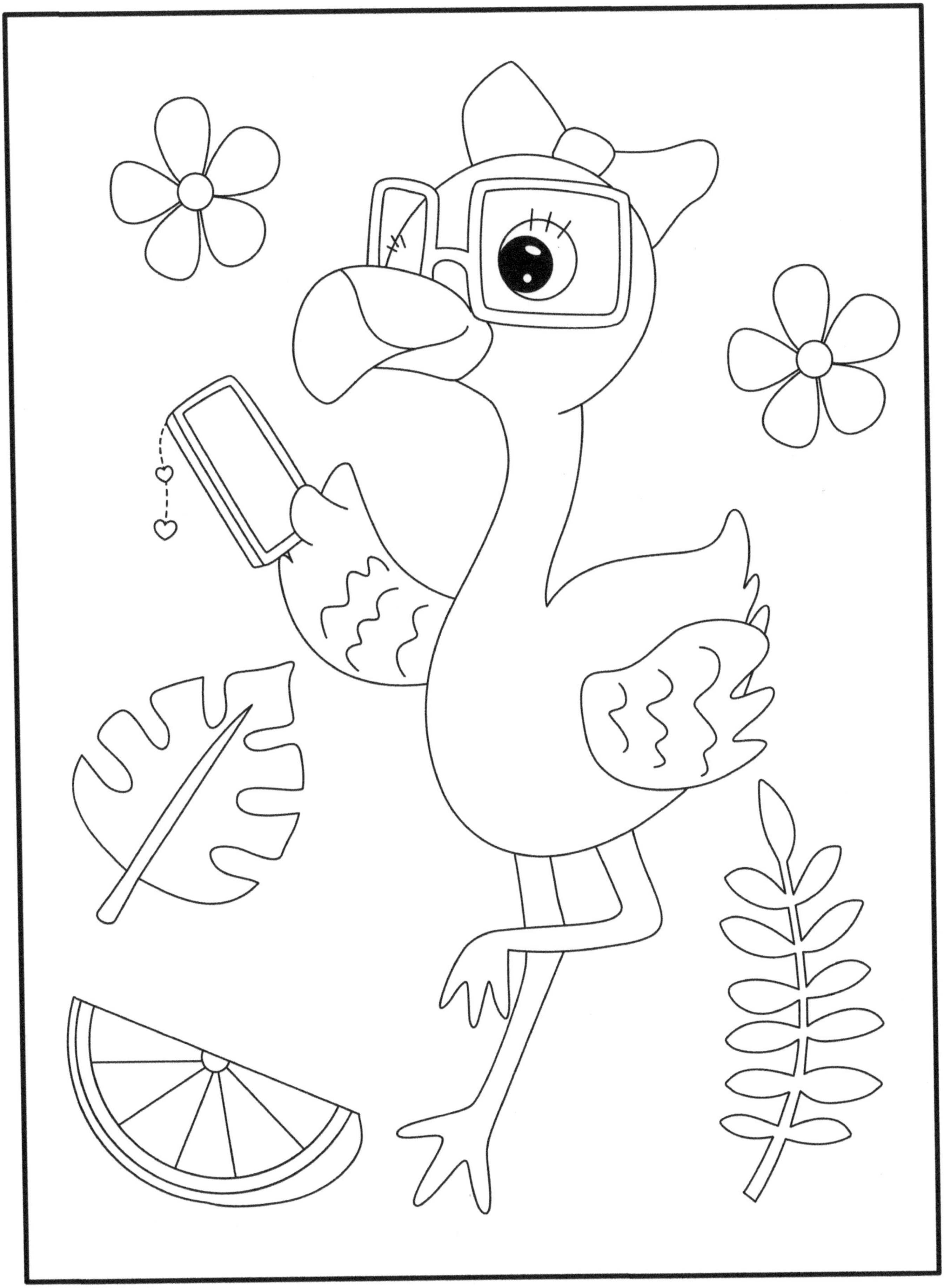

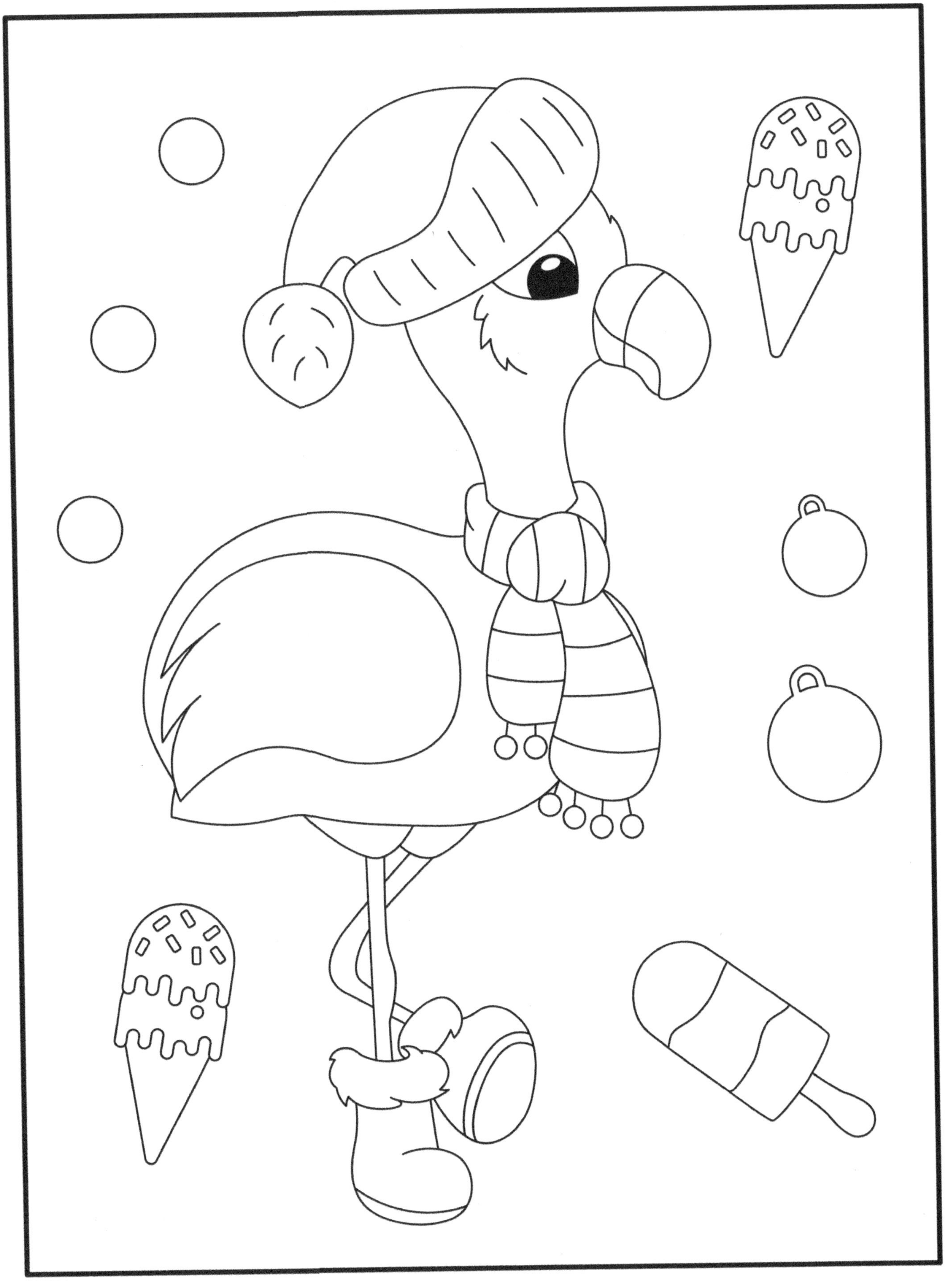

Made in the USA
Las Vegas, NV
10 December 2024

13776669R10037